MW01173429

The Time Traveller's CookBook

The Time Traveller's Cookbook
First Published 2024

ISBN: 978-1-7635947-0-8

Contents

Introduction

As a cinematographer and editor, my job has taken me to some very interesting places. Places not many people get to see. As a passionate historian and cook, I often found myself gravitating to kitchens and cook fires. Old women whom I had no common language with other than the food itself. When I was able, I'd ask questions. If I understood enough, I'd write things down. When allowed to participate I had the back of my hand slapped with wooden spoons more than once for stirring a pot the wrong way... or too fast... or not enough.

I never intended to write a cookbook. It was for me. Bringing a recipe home from somewhere incredible was as good as footage. Better in some ways. To smell and taste those things again was like a portal to a memory. I wanted to be able to revisit those villages and communities and tribes whenever I wanted. And it worked.

So I started thinking about places I couldn't go. Places even further out of reach... the ancient past. Could I uncover the forgotten tastes and smells of history? I went to the metaphorical hardware store, bought a shovel made of dreams and began to dig.

The Time Traveller's Cookbook is more than just random recipes collected during my travels. It's also a heavily researched culinary journey into the forgotten worlds of our ancestors.

That being said, I have taken some liberties for the sake of modern convenience. Times change and some ingredients used commonly today weren't available to those that lived in those places in ancient times. So I've tried to find a blend and walk the line between historical fact, tradition, and modern availability, to create recipes that are as true to their origins as possible while not being impossible to find the ingredients for.

Many of the recipes are simple to make. Some are a little more complicated. I wanted to illustrate a broad range that didn't just show the meals adorning the tables of Pharaohs and kings, but those enjoyed by commoners too. And I'm proud of the balance I found.

The biggest surprise to many is just how familiar most of these smells and tastes are to us today. A great many of these ancient recipes remain with us in some form. As a species, it seems that we worked out what we liked early on, and many of our currently enjoyed favourites have literally stood the test of time.

That being said, there are more than a few surprises.

For me, the Time Traveller's Cookbook is a window to forgotten worlds. A way to transport yourself into the cultures and homes and lives of long forgotten people whose tastes were as individual as yours and mine.

I hope you enjoy creating these recipes as much as I've enjoyed discovering them. So before ado's can be in any way furthered, fire up your flux capacitors. Let's get this thing up to 88mph.

Matt Connor

Ancient Egypt

Ah.. Ancient Egypt. Everyone loves ancient Egypt, right?! Lets start big. The Pyramids, the Sphinx… a mythical world of Gods and Pharaohs. We all know that stuff. But what the hell did they eat?
Well, one of the key features of Ancient Egyptian cuisine was the importance of bread. From the pharaohs to the common people, bread was a staple food in Ancient Egypt and was made from a variety of grains such as wheat, barley, and millet. The bread was often served with a variety of accompaniments, including vegetables, meat, and cheese.

Which vegetables? Some of the most commonly used vegetables included onions, garlic, lettuce, cucumbers, beans, and lentils.
Meat was primarily consumed by the wealthier classes. Beef, lamb… goat, as well as more exotic meats such as gazelle, antelope, and ostrich.

Fish and seafood were also a popular part of Ancient Egyptian cuisine, due to the country's proximity to the Nile River and the Mediterranean Sea. Fish was often cooked in a variety of ways, including grilling, frying, and boiling, and was sometimes preserved by salting and drying.

Herbs and spices like cumin, coriander, dill and mint were widely used.

The staple grain was Emmer (or Farro), which resembles brown rice and was a major source of protein, vitamins, minerals and antioxidants. Not easily available in most countries, it can be substituted with Spelt, a related and more common grain.
If you want to experience the wonders of Ancient Egyptian cuisine for yourself, get some fava beans… they loved fava beens and put them in most things. Also beer! Whatever recipe you are interested in making, be sure to serve it with beer.
They had it with every single meal. Even breakfast.

So lets start there.

DID YOU KNOW...

The Egyptians loved a good game! They enjoyed a variety of board games, including Senet, which involved strategy and a bit of luck, and Mehen, a race game with a serpent-shaped board. These games transcended social class and were played by people of all ages.

Ta'amia (Egyptian Falafel)

SERVES
2

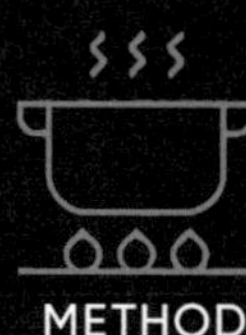

METHOD
DEEP FRY

TIME
60 mins

DIFFICULTY
4/10

INGREDIENTS:

2 cups of dried fava beans, soaked overnight
1/2 cup Fresh parsley
1/2 cup Fresh coriander
1/2 cup Fresh dill
1 small onion, chopped
3 garlic cloves, minced
1 tsp baking powder
1 tsp ground cumin
1 tsp ground coriander
1 tsp salt
1 tsp ground pepper

Vegetable oil, for frying
serve with tahini, lemon and pita bread

Ever craved falafel but wished it was lighter, brighter? Then ditch the usual chickpea fritters and explore Ta'amia, the original falafel from Egypt! Imagine golden brown pockets bursting with fluffy fava beans instead of chickpeas. Fresh herbs like parsley and cilantro peek through every bite, adding pops of colour and freshness. Each mouthful is a delightful contrast - crispy on the outside, soft and flavorful on the inside.

This isn't a new flavour, it's a taste of history. Ta'amia has been a favourite Egyptian street food for centuries, a testament to their culinary genius. Simple, fresh ingredients come together to create a symphony of savoury goodness, perfect for a light lunch or a satisfying snack. It's a vegetarian option everyone can enjoy, a delicious adventure waiting to be savoured.

1. Drain the soaked fava beans and rinse them well. Remove the outer
skins by rubbing the beans with your hands.
2. In a food processor, combine the fava beans, onion, garlic, cumin, frsh parsley, coriander, and salt. Pulse until the mixture forms a coarse paste.
3. transfer to bowl and mix in ground cumin, ground coriander, baking powder, salt and pepper.
4. Cover the mixture and let it rest for at least 30 minutes.
5. Heat the oil in a deep-fryer or a heavy pot over medium heat.
6. Form the mixture into small balls or patties and fry until golden brown.
7. Serve the ta'amia hot with tahini sauce, lemon and pita bread. Enjoy!

QUOTE...

"To have peace there must be strife; both are part of the structure of the world and requirements"

-Ancient Egyptian Proverb

Ful Medames

SERVES	METHOD	TIME	DIFFICULTY
4	BOIL	3 Hours	4/10

Ever wonder what Egyptian street food tasted like in ancient times? Forget fancy feasts for Pharaohs - the real fuel for the working class was Ful Medames. This fava bean stew is a flavour explosion in a bowl. Imagine creamy beans, slow-cooked until they practically melt in your mouth. A hit of lemon juice cuts through the richness, while spices like cumin add a warm, earthy kick. Smooth beans with pops of fresh tomato and parsley, Ful Medames has been a breakfast and lunch staple for thousands of years. It's a celebration of fresh, simple ingredients that'll keep you energized all day long. Plus, you can customize it with your favourite toppings - a fun way to explore the flavours of Egypt right from your kitchen.

INGREDIENTS:

450g (1lb) Dried fava beans

2 garlic cloves, minced

1/4 cup olive oil

1/4 cup lemon juice

1tsp Ground cumin

Salt and pepper, to taste

Garnishes: chopped tomatoes, chopped onions, chopped parsley, thin lemon slices and zest, boiled eggs, and pita bread.

1. Rinse the fava beans and soak them in water overnight.
2. Drain the beans and rinse them again.
3. In a large pot, cover the beans with water and bring to a boil.
4. Reduce the heat and simmer the beans for 2-3 hours, or until they are tender.
5. Drain the beans and mash them with a fork or potato masher.
6. In a small bowl, whisk together the minced garlic, olive oil, lemon juice, cumin, salt, and pepper.
7. Add the garlic and oil mixture to the mashed beans and stir until well combined.
8. Transfer the Ful Medames to a serving bowl and garnish with chopped tomatoes, onions, parsley, lemon zest, boiled eggs, and pita bread.

WOULD YOU RATHER...

Be a Pharoh of Egypt or an Emperor of Rome?

SERVES
4

METHOD
GRILL

TIME
35 mins

DIFFICULTY
3/10

INGREDIENTS:

For the kofta:
450g (1lb) Ground beef or lamb
1/2 cup chopped onion
2 cloves garlic, minced
1/2 cup chopped fresh parsley
1/2 cup chopped fresh cilantro
1/2 tsp Ground cumin
1/2 tsp Ground coriander
1/2 tsp paprika
1/2 tsp salt
1/4 tsp Black pepper

For the dipping sauce:
1 cup plain yogurt
1/4 cup chopped fresh mint
1/4 cup chopped fresh cilantro
1/4tsp. salt

Fire up the grill for a taste of an Egyptian classic! Kofta Mishwiya isn't your average skewered meat. These juicy lamb kebabs are a symphony of smoky, savoury flavours passed down through generations. Imagine tender, seasoned ground lamb grilled to perfection. But the magic lies in the burst of freshness. Chopped parsley and mint mingle with the richness of the meat in every bite. Smoky char mingles with juicy lamb and pops of fresh herbs - a true dance on the palate.

Fresh lamb is key, but the real secret weapon is the unique blend of herbs and spices. Parsley and mint add a burst of freshness, while cumin and coriander create a depth of flavour. Unlike countless other kebabs, this Egyptian dish stands out. It's hearty yet refreshing, perfect on its own or nestled in warm pita bread. Plus, it's surprisingly easy to make, bringing the taste of Egyptian street food right to your backyard.

1. In a large bowl, combine the ground beef or lamb, chopped onion, minced garlic, parsley, cilantro, cumin, coriander, paprika, salt, and black pepper. Mix well.
2. Divide the meat mixture into 16-20 small balls.
3. Thread 3-4 meatballs onto skewers, leaving a small space between each one.
4. Preheat a grill or grill pan to medium-high heat.
5. Grill the kofta skewers for 8-10 minutes, turning occasionally, until the meat is cooked through and charred in places.
6. While the kofta is cooking, prepare the dipping sauce by combining the yogurt, mint, cilantro, and salt in a small bowl. Mix well.
7. Serve the kofta hot with the dipping sauce on the side.

SERVES

6

METHOD

PAN

TIME

20 mins

DIFFICULTY

2/10

Craving a healthy nibble with a historical twist? Discover Dukkah, an ancient Egyptian snack bursting with flavor. Picture toasted nuts and seeds blending almond, hazelnut, and sesame crunch, with hints of cumin and coriander. Drizzled with olive oil, each bite offers a delightful mix of textures and savory goodness.

Dukkah isn't just a snack; it's a culinary tradition dating back centuries. Enjoyed after meals by Egyptians for generations, it's now yours to savor. Dip pita bread or veggies into this versatile delight, exploring Egyptian cuisine from your own kitchen. With endless possibilities for nuts, seeds, and spices, Dukkah promises a tasty journey through history.

1. Toast the Nuts and Seeds: In a dry skillet over medium heat, separately toast the hazelnuts or almonds, sesame seeds, coriander seeds, cumin seeds, and fennel seeds until fragrant. Be careful not to burn them, and stir frequently.
Grind the Mixture: Allow the toasted ingredients to cool. Once cooled, grind them together in a food processor or using a mortar and pestle until you achieve a coarse, textured blend.
2. Seasoning: Add salt (if desired) and black peppercorns to the mixture, giving it a gentle stir to combine evenly.
3. Serve: Dukkah is typically served with bread or flatbreads. To enjoy, dip the bread in olive oil and then into the Dukkah mixture.

INGREDIENTS:

* 1 cup hazelnuts or almonds

* 1/2 cup sesame seeds

* 2 tbsp coriander seeds

* 1 tbsp cumin seeds

* 1 tsp fennel seeds

* 1 tsp salt (optional)

* 1/2 tsp black peppercorns

Serve with Crusty bread and olive oil

MODERN EGYPT

In ancient Egypt, the cuisine was largely influenced by the ingredients that were available at the time, as well as religious practices. Bread, beer, and vegetables such as onions, garlic, and beans were the staples of the diet, while meat was a luxury reserved for the wealthy. Spices such as cumin, coriander, and cinnamon were used to add flavour, and honey was used as a sweetener.

Over time, Egyptian cuisine has been influenced by various cultures, including Persian, Greek, Roman, Ottoman, and Arab. These influences have led to the introduction of new ingredients and cooking techniques, as well as changes in dietary restrictions.

In modern times, Egyptian cuisine is a blend of traditional dishes and global trends. Of course fast-food chains have made their way into the country too, but traditional flavours and dishes still play an important role. Popular dishes include koshari, a mix of rice, lentils, and macaroni topped with fried onions and tomato sauce, and ful medames, a dish made from fava beans that is often eaten for breakfast. Grilled meats and seafood are also popular, and desserts such as baklava and kunafa are enjoyed. Changes in agriculture and food production have lead to an increase in the cost of bread and a decrease in its availability which is sad to see considering the huge role it played in their past.

Overall, Egyptian cuisine has come a long way from its ancient roots. While traditional flavours and dishes still hold an important place, modern influences have led to the introduction of new ingredients and cooking techniques. But some popular stuff today has simply stood the test of time. If they loved it then... and they still love it now, that's how you know it's good.

Lets check out some uniquely Egyptian foods people are enjoying today.

Mahshi Betinjan (Part 1)

SERVES
4

METHOD
POT

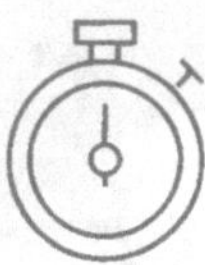

TIME
20 mins

DIFFICULTY
7/10

INGREDIENTS:

PICKLING

10 small eggplants (preferably baby or small Italian eggplants)

4 cups water

2 cups white vinegar

2 tbsp salt

1 head garlic, peeled and smashed

1 tbsp whole black peppercorns

2 bay leaves

More ingredients in part 2

Mahshi Betinjan, also known as stuffed eggplant, is a classic Middle Eastern dish that's flavorful and hearty. The pickling adds an extra depth of flavour to the eggplants before they're stuffed and cooked. Here's a traditional recipe for Mahshi Betinjan enjoyed in Egypt.

1. Prepare the Eggplant: Wash the eggplants. Using a sharp spoon, scoop out the flesh of the eggplants, leaving a 1/4-inch border around the edges.

2. In a large pot, combine water, vinegar, salt, smashed garlic, black peppercorns, and bay leaves. Bring the mixture to a boil, then reduce to a simmer.

3. Submerge the hollowed eggplants in the pickling solution. Simmer for about 10 minutes, or until the eggplants are slightly tender but not fully cooked.

4. Remove the eggplants from the pickling solution and let them drain on a wire rack or paper towels. Allow them to cool completely before stuffing.

Now for the stuffing!!! Jump over to the next page.

DID YOU KNOW...
Modern Music Scene: While traditional music remains important, Egypt boasts a thriving contemporary music scene. Popular genres include Mahragan, a fast-paced electronic dance music with roots in working-class neighbourhoods, and Indie rock with Western influences.

Mahshi Betinjan (Part 2)

SERVES
4

METHOD
POT

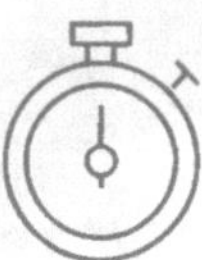

TIME
2 hours

DIFFICULTY
7/10

INGREDIENTS:

1 cup medium-grain rice, rinsed
1/2 cup chopped onion
1/2 cup chopped fresh parsley
1/4 cup chopped fresh mint
1/4 cup chopped pine nuts, toasted
1 small tomato, chopped
1 tbsp olive oil
1/2 tsp ground allspice
1/4 tsp ground cinnamon
1/4 tsp salt
Black pepper to taste
4 cups vegetable broth or water
1 tbsp tomato paste (optional)
Lemon wedges, for serving (optional)

1. Prepare the Stuffing: In a large bowl, combine the rinsed rice, onion, parsley, mint, pine nuts, chopped tomato, olive oil, allspice, cinnamon, salt, and black pepper.

2. Stuff the Eggplant: Squeeze any excess moisture from the reserved eggplant flesh and chop it into small pieces. Add the chopped eggplant flesh and mix well.

3. Stuff and Seal the Eggplant: Spoon the stuffing mixture into the hollowed-out eggplants, packing it gently but firmly. Use toothpicks to recombine eggplant halves.

4. Cooking: Place the stuffed eggplants upright in a large pot or Dutch oven. Pour in the vegetable broth or water, making sure it reaches at least halfway up the eggplants. Add the tomato paste (if using) to the broth. Bring to a boil, then reduce heat to low, cover, and simmer for about 45 minutes to 1 hour, or until the rice is cooked through and the eggplants are tender.

5. Serve: Carefully remove the cooked eggplants from the pot with a slotted spoon and transfer them to a serving platter. Spoon some of the remaining broth around the eggplants. Serve warm with lemon wedges.

QUOTE...

"Denial ain't just a river in Egypt."
-Mark Twain

HAMAM MAHSHI

SERVES
4

METHOD
POT

TIME
1 hour 15 mins

DIFFICULTY
5/10

Firstly, don't just go down to the park and bag a pigeon please. Tender quail or spatchcock... squab or even Cornish hens are great. Use them. They're tasty. The magic lies within: a fragrant stuffing of fluffy rice or freekeh, aromatic onions, and warm spices. Each mouthful a delightful contrast of textures and flavors.

This dish is both luxurious and approachable, perfect for any occasion. Plus, the versatile stuffing allows for experimentation, making it a fun exploration of Egyptian flavors at home.

1. Rinse your birds (remove any feathers and organs if you ignored me and got yourself a park pigeon). Wash them well and pat dry.
2. In a pan, sauté the chopped onion in butter until it turns golden brown.
3. Add the rice, cumin, salt, and pepper to the pan and stir well.
4. Fill the birds with the rice mixture.
5. Close the opening of each bird with a toothpick or kitchen string to prevent the stuffing from falling out during cooking.
6. In a pot, heat the chicken broth and add the stuffed birds.
7. Cover the pot and let it simmer for about 1 hour, or until the birdss are cooked through.
8. Serve the hamam mahshi hot with some of the cooking broth, and enjoy!

Note: You can also add some herbs, such as parsley or dill, to the stuffing mixture to enhance the flavour.

INGREDIENTS:

4 pigeons (quail or spatchcock)

1 cup of white rice

1 onion, finely chopped

2 tbsp of butter

1 tsp of cumin

Salt and pepper, to taste

2 cups of chicken broth

WOULD YOU RATHER...
Be Locked in the Great Pyramid overnight or be on a sinking Nile cruise?

FETEER (EGYTIAN PIE)

SERVES
4

METHOD
POT

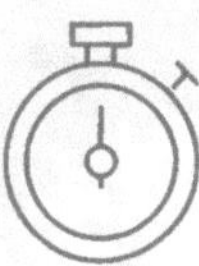

TIME
1 hour 15 mins

DIFFICULTY
5/10

INGREDIENTS:

3 cups all-purpose flour
1/4 tsp salt
1 tbsp sugar
1 tbsp instant yeast
1/2 cup warm water
1/2 cup vegetable oil
450g (1lb) ground beef or lamb
1 large onion, chopped
2 cloves garlic, minced
1tbsp ground cumin
1 tbsp paprika
1 tsp ground coriander
Salt and black pepper to taste
1/2 cup crumbled feta cheese (optional)
1 egg, beaten

1. In a large bowl, whisk together the flour, salt, sugar, and instant yeast. Gradually add the warm water and vegetable oil, mixing until a dough forms.
2. Turn the dough out onto a floured surface and knead for about 10 minutes, or until smooth and elastic.
3. Cover the dough with a damp towel and let it rest for 30 minutes.
4. Preheat the oven to 400°F (200°C).
5. In a large skillet, cook the ground beef or lamb over medium heat until browned, breaking it up with a spatula as it cooks.
6. Add the chopped onion and garlic to the skillet and cook until the onion is soft and translucent.
7. Stir in the cumin, paprika, coriander, salt, and black pepper, and cook for another minute or two.
8. Remove the skillet from the heat and let the filling cool slightly.
9. Divide the dough into 4 equal portions. Roll out each portion on a floured surface to a thin circle, about 12 inches in diameter.
10. Spread a quarter of the meat mixture over each circle of dough, leaving a border around the edge.
11. If using, sprinkle a quarter of the crumbled feta cheese over the meat mixture.
12. Fold the edges of the dough over the filling, pinching and twisting to seal.
13. Brush each feteer with beaten egg.
14. Bake the feteer on a baking sheet for 20-25 minutes, or until golden brown and crispy.
15. Serve the feteer hot, cut into wedges.

UMM ALI

SERVES
4

METHOD
POT

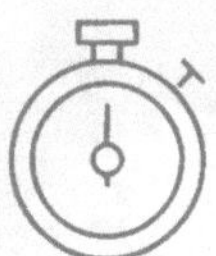

TIME
45 mins

DIFFICULTY
3/10

Umm Ali, a cherished Egyptian dessert, transcends the ordinary. Imagine warm, gooey pastry cradling creamy custard, nuts, and raisins. Each bite bursts with contrasting textures: crisp pastry against smooth custard, punctuated by crunchy nuts and sweet raisins.

Its magic lies in the unexpected. Flaky pastry meets creamy, spiced custard, creating a flavor and texture sensation. Nuts add richness, while raisins provide pops of sweetness. Unlike bread puddings, Umm Ali focuses on simple comfort. It's luxurious yet down-homey, ending a meal perfectly. Embrace the indulgence – a symphony of textures and flavors in a bowl, waiting to be shared.

1. Preheat the Oven: Preheat your oven to 350°F (180°C).
2. Prepare the Bread: Place the torn croissants or puff pastry pieces in a baking dish.
3. Create the Filling: In a saucepan, heat the milk, heavy cream, sugar, nuts, coconut, vanilla extract, cinnamon, and a pinch of salt over medium heat. Stir until the sugar dissolves, and the mixture is well combined. Do not boil.
4. Pour Over the Bread: Pour the milk mixture over the torn croissants or puff pastry in the baking dish, ensuring an even distribution.
5. Bake to Perfection: Bake in the preheated oven for 25-30 minutes or until the top is golden brown and the pudding is set.
6. Serve: Allow Umm Ali to cool slightly before serving. Optionally, dust with powdered sugar.

INGREDIENTS:

4 croissants or puff pastry, torn into pieces
4 cups whole milk
1 cup heavy cream
1/2 cup sugar
1/2 cup mixed nuts (such as almonds, pistachios, and walnuts), chopped
1/4 cup desiccated coconut
1 tsp vanilla extract
Pinch of cinnamon
Pinch of salt
Powdered sugar for dusting (optional)

Ancient Mesopotamia

What do you think of when you think about Ancient Mesopotamian? The birthplace of civilisation? Inventors of the wheel? Winged bulls and Ziggurats? Well, it's where writing began... so it's where humanity's oldest recipes come from too. Compared to other cultures like the Celts (who didn't write down anything... ever), we actually know a fair bit about the Mesopotamian diet and cuisine. Diverse as the culture itself, their menu was filled with unique flavours and ingredients that will take your taste buds on a journey through history.

Barley and wheat were used for bread, porridge, and stews.
Lamb, beef and goat were prominent but duck and gazelle were also popular. Being between the Tigris and Euphrates rivers, fish was plentiful and there was obviously even more seafood in the coastal regions.
As for vegetables, onions, garlic, leeks, and lettuce were most commonly used, often paired with meat or grains to create hearty stews and soups.
Fruits such as dates, figs, pomegranates and apples were also commonly eaten, either fresh or dried. These fruits were used in a variety of dishes, including desserts and savoury stews.

Mesopotamian cuisine was also known for its use of herbs and spices, including coriander, cumin, and dill. These spices were used to add depth and complexity to dishes and to preserve food.
Some of the most famous dishes of Ancient Mesopotamian cuisine include Pottage, a stew made with grains, meat, and vegetables, and Shourpa, a soup made with lamb or beef and a variety of vegetables.
If you're looking to experience the flavours of Ancient Mesopotamia for yourself, why not try recreating some of these classic dishes in your kitchen? Not only will you be exploring an ancient cuisine, but you'll also be experiencing a piece of history in every bite.

DID YOU KNOW...

Education for All: While scribes and scholars came from elite families, Mesopotamian society offered a surprising level of education. Schools called "edubba," existed to train both young boys and girls in cuneiform writing, literature, mathematics, and even law.

Sour Milk Cheese

SERVES	METHOD	TIME	DIFFICULTY
1	BOWL	15 mins	2/10

INGREDIENTS:

1 cup sour milk (you can make sour milk by letting regular milk ferment slightly)

1/2 cup soft cheese or curds (similar to a simple farmer's cheese)

Barley flatbread or unleavened bread (common in Mesopotamian times)

Honey or dates for sweetening (optional)

This breakfast provides a unique glimpse into the dairy-centric elements of ancient Mesopotamian cuisine, where sour milk and simple cheeses were consumed. The use of barley flatbread as a staple reflects the grains prevalent in the region. It sounds so much worse than it is. Sour milk cheese is basically like Cottage cheese but better.

Note: This can take 24 hours to sour if doing it authentically. But if you want to buy sourcream and cottage cheese you can make a quick version in no time.

1. Prepare the Sour Milk: Allow regular milk to sit at room temperature for around 24 hours to achieve the mildly sour flavour (longer depending on how sour you like it), it will also thicken slightly.
2. Make Soft Cheese or Curds: Prepare a simple soft cheese by curdling milk with a small amount of vinegar or another acidic substance. Strain to obtain curds.
3. Serve: Spread the soft cheese or curds on the barley flatbread. Accompany it with a side of sour milk.

Sweeten to Taste: If desired, add a touch of sweetness with honey or chopped dates.

This one might sound a little off-putting to some at first, but it's actually very good. Try it out and see for yourself.

QUOTE...

"Choose to live and choose to love; choose to rise above and give back what you yourself were given."

-Epic of Gilgamesh

SERVES

4

METHOD

POT

TIME

2 hours

DIFFICULTY

4/10

Shirku, a hearty stew rich in history and flavor. This timeless dish combines tender cubes of lamb or beef with a vibrant vegetables with the freshness of mint and coriander. Beyond its historical appeal, Shirku is a dish of pure comfort. The slow simmering coaxes out the essence of each ingredient, resulting in a rich and deeply satisfying broth. Served alongside warm flatbread or fluffy rice, Shirku is a feast fit for a king ...or you! Tonight!

Note: This can take 24 hours to sour if doing it authentically. But if you want to buy sourcream and cottage cheese you can make a quick version in no time.

1. In a large pot or dutch oven, heat the olive oil over medium-high heat. Add the cubed meat and cook until browned on all sides, about 5-7 minutes.
2. Add the onion and garlic to the pot and sauté until softened, about 2-3 minutes.
3. Pour in the beef broth and bring to a simmer. Add the chopped vegetables and herbs and season with salt and pepper.
4. Reduce the heat to low and cover the pot. Allow the stew to simmer for 1-2 hours, or until the meat is tender and the vegetables are cooked through.
5. Adjust the seasoning as needed and serve the shirku hot with flatbread or rice.

INGREDIENTS:

450g (1lb) lamb or beef, cubed
1 onion, chopped
2 garlic cloves, minced
2 tbsp olive oil
2 cups beef broth
1 cup chopped carrots
1 cup chopped turnips
1 cup chopped leeks
1 cup chopped celery
1 tbsp chopped fresh mint
1 tbsp chopped fresh parsley
1 tbsp chopped fresh cilantro
Salt and pepper, to taste

WOULD YOU RATHER...
Be a very wealthy citizen in ancient Mesopotamia or a middle-class person today?

SERVES

4

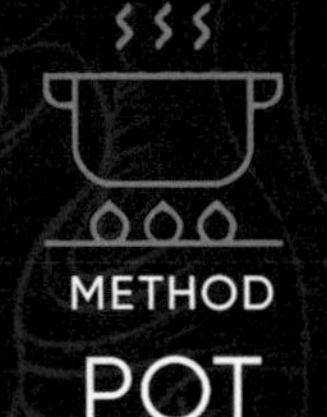

METHOD

POT

TIME

2 hours

DIFFICULTY

5/10

Imagine a bowl overflowing with melt-in-your-mouth lamb or mutton, simmered in a tangy, aromatic broth. But Sikbaj offers more than just savoury richness. Plump raisins and tart apricots nestle amongst the meat, creating a delightful play of textures and sweetness. Each spoonful transports you, the richness of the meat counterbalanced by the fruit's vibrancy and the broth's subtle tang. It's a flavour odyssey for your taste buds.

INGREDIENTS:

450g (1lb) beef or lamb stew meat, cut into bite-sized pieces
1 onion, diced
2 garlic cloves, minced
2 tomatoes, diced
2 bell peppers diced
1 tsp ground cumin
1 tsp paprika
1 tsp coriander
1/2 tsp turmeric
1/2 tsp cinnamon
2 cups beef or lamb broth
1/2 cup dried apricots, chopped
1/2 cup dried prunes, chopped
1/4 cup honey
Salt and pepper, to taste
Fresh cilantro, chopped, for garnish

1. Heat a large pot over medium-high heat. Add the stew meat and cook until browned on all sides, about 5 minutes. Remove the meat from the pot and set aside.
2. Add the onion and garlic to the pot and cook until the onion is translucent, about 5 minutes. Add the tomatoes and bell peppers and cook for another 5 minutes.
3. Add the cumin, paprika, coriander, turmeric, and cinnamon to the pot and stir until fragrant, about 1 minute.
4. Return the meat to the pot and add the broth. Bring to a boil, then reduce the heat to low and simmer for 1 hour.
5. Add the dried apricots, dried prunes, and honey to the pot and stir to combine. Continue to simmer for another 30 minutes, or until the meat is tender and the sauce has thickened.
6. Season with salt and pepper to taste.
7. Serve hot, garnished with chopped fresh cilantro. Enjoy with rice, couscous, or bread.

For presentation, Sprinkle fresh cilantro or parsley on top of the dish to add a pop of color and freshness.
Top the dish with some crispy fried tortilla strips or croutons for added texture.
Serve with a side of lime wedges

Halwa Semida

SERVES	METHOD	TIME	DIFFICULTY
4	PAN	35 mins	2/10

This pudding celebrates the inherent sweetness of grains and the subtle perfume of spices. Creamy semolina, speckled with toasted nuts and plump raisins. A sprinkle of warming cinnamon or cardamom adds an exotic touch.

1. In a saucepan, bring the milk to a boil over medium-high heat.

Puddings are everywhere, but this Mesopotamian Semolina Pudding shines for its focus on simple, ancient ingredients and subtle sweetness. Nourishing and satisfying, it's the perfect light and flavourful way to end any meal.

2. Reduce the heat to low and add the semolina, stirring constantly to prevent lumps from forming.
3. Cook the semolina for 10-15 minutes, or until it has thickened to a pudding-like consistency.
4. Add the honey, cinnamon, and dried fruits to the saucepan, stirring to combine.
5. Cook the pudding for an additional 5 minutes, or until the fruits are soft and the pudding is fully sweetened.
6. Remove the saucepan from the heat and transfer the pudding to serving dishes.
7. Allow the pudding to cool for 10-15 minutes before sprinkling with chopped almonds (if using).
8. Serve warm or chilled.

INGREDIENTS:

1 cup semolina

4 cups milk

1 cup honey

1 tsp cinnamon

1/2 cup dried dates or raisins

1/4 cup chopped almonds (optional)

Modern Iraq

Over time, Iraqi cuisine has been influenced by various cultures, including Persian, Turkish, and Arab. These influences have mixed things up a bit. New ingredients and spices, as well as changes in cooking techniques, have brought the Iraqi menu a long way from the days of Mesopotamia. But, as we've seen before, there are still some traditional classics that have stood the test of time. That's a recurring theme I loved when putting this book together. Not only do we get to discover what our ancestors used to eat in the distant past, but we also get to discover that their tastes weren't so different to ours. There's a connection in that.

Popular dishes in modern Iraqi cooking include biryani, a flavourful rice dish with meat and vegetables, and dolma, stuffed grape leaves or vegetables. The use of spices such as cinnamon, cumin, and coriander add depth and complexity to many dishes, but one of the unique aspects of Iraqi cuisine is the use of sour flavours, such as in the popular dish masgouf, a grilled fish dish marinated in tamarind sauce. The use of sour ingredients is also seen in soups and stews, such as the tangy tomato-based dish called kubba hamuth.

Despite modern influences, many families continue to use family recipes that have been passed down for generations, and food plays an important role in Iraqi culture and hospitality. Overall, Iraqi cuisine is a delightful mix of ancient and modern flavours, with unique dishes and spices that set it apart from other cuisines. Try out some of these recipes and if you like them please explore the flavours of Iraq more on your own. I was surprised when I first tried these wonderful dishes. And they are recipes that I've found myself going back to again and again.

DID YOU KNOW...

The Poetry Powerhouse: Iraq has a long and celebrated history of poetry. Poetry readings and competitions are still common, and Iraqis hold a deep appreciation for the written word. Even everyday conversations can be infused with poetic language and metaphors.

KHUBZ & BIGILLA

SERVES
4

METHOD
OVEN

TIME
1 hour 30mins

DIFFICULTY
4/10

INGREDIENTS:

Ingredients for Khubz:
3 cups all-purpose flour
1 tbsp instant yeast
1 tsp sugar
1 tsp salt
1 cup luke warm water
1/4 cup olive oil
1 egg, beaten

Ingredients for Bigilla:
2 cups cooked fava beans (or 1 can of fava beans)
3 cloves of garlic
1/2 tsp cumin
1/2 tsp salt
1/4 cup lemon juice
1/4 cup olive oil
1/4 cup water

Travel the vibrant streets of Iraq with Khubz and Bigilla, a dynamic duo that tantalizes taste buds. Forget greasy fare – this is an explosion of fresh flavours and textures.
Imagine warm, pillowy Khubz, a flatbread unlike any other, spread with Bigilla, a vibrant green revelation of creamy fava bean puree kissed with olive oil, lemon juice, and a touch of cumin. Earthy, citrusy and smokey... So Good. .

1. In a large bowl, mix together the flour, yeast, sugar, and salt.
2. Add the lukewarm water and olive oil, and mix until a dough forms.
3. Knead the dough on a floured surface for 5-10 minutes, until smooth and elastic.
4. Place the dough in a lightly oiled bowl, cover with a damp towel, and let rise in a warm place for 1 hour.
5. Preheat the oven to 450°F.
6. Divide the dough into 8 equal pieces, and roll each piece into a thin circle.
7. Place the circles on a baking sheet lined with parchment paper, and brush with beaten egg.
8. Bake for 8-10 minutes, until golden brown and puffed up.

Directions for Bigilla:
1. In a food processor, blend the fava beans, garlic, cumin, and salt until smooth.
2. Slowly add the lemon juice, olive oil, and water, and blend until the mixture is creamy.
3. Transfer the bigilla to a bowl, and serve with the khubz.
Enjoy your delicious Iraqi khubz and bigilla!

QUOTE...

"The words of Iraqi poets, both ancient and modern, resonate with a profound love for their land, a deep well of resilience, and a yearning for peace."

- Nawal al-Saadawi

TASHREEB

SERVES
4

METHOD
POT

TIME
1 hour 20 mins

DIFFICULTY
4/10

Imagine A rich, savoury broth, warming spices, tender, slow-simmered meat... Nestled within the flavorful depths are pieces of fluffy flatbread, each morsel a delightful contrast – It's a culinary hug in a bowl, perfect for cozy nights in.
While stews with bread are found worldwide, Tashreeb stands out for its simplicity and resourcefulness. It's a dish that transforms leftover bread into a hearty and satisfying meal. Plus, its versatility allows for exploration with spices, vegetables, and meats, making it a great way to use up leftovers and create something new every time.

INGREDIENTS:

450g (1lb) lamb or beef, cut into small cubes
2 onions, chopped
3 garlic cloves, minced
1 tsp ground turmeric
1 tsp ground cumin
1 tsp paprika
Salt and pepper, to taste
8-10 cups water or beef broth
1 large piece of Iraqi bread or pita, torn into small pieces
1 tbsp tomato paste
2 tbsp chopped fresh parsley
2 tbsp chopped fresh cilantro
2 tbsp chopped fresh mint
Lemon wedges, for serving

1. In a large pot, sauté the onions and garlic until softened. Add the meat and brown on all sides.
2. Add the turmeric, cumin, paprika, salt, and pepper to the pot and stir to coat the meat. Cook for 1-2 minutes.
3. Pour in the water or beef broth and bring to a boil. Reduce the heat to low and simmer for 1-2 hours until the meat is tender.
4. Remove the meat from the pot and shred it using two forks.
5. Add the torn bread to the pot and stir well to combine. Cook for 5-10 minutes until the bread has absorbed most of the liquid.
6. Add the shredded meat back to the pot along with the tomato paste, parsley, cilantro, and mint. Stir well to combine and cook for an additional 10-15 minutes.
7. Serve the tashreeb hot, with lemon wedges on the side for squeezing over the top.

Enjoy the delicious flavours and comforting warmth of this traditional Iraqi dish!

WOULD YOU RATHER...

Visit the ancient ruins of Babylon or Visit Uruk and Ur?

MASGOUF

SERVES
4

METHOD
OVEN

TIME
40mins

DIFFICULTY
3/10

INGREDIENTS:

2-3 whole carp or tilapia fish, cleaned and gutted
1 cup vegetable oil
1 tbsp ground turmeric
1 tbsp ground cumin
1 tbsp paprika
1 tbsp salt
1 tsp black pepper
4 garlic cloves, minced
1/4 cup lemon juice
1/4 cup white vinegar
1/4 cup chopped fresh parsley
1/4 cup chopped fresh cilantro

Travel the Tigris River with Masgouf, a legendary Iraqi dish. Unlike ordinary grilled fish, Masgouf offers a sensory experience, a celebration of simplicity that lets nature's flavours sing.
Flakey Carp beautifully infused with a subtle smokiness. A squeeze of lemon and a sprinkle of fragrant paprika add vibrant notes. Each bite is a journey back in time, a taste of the dish that has nourished generations of Iraqis.

.

1. Preheat the grill or oven to 450°F.
2. In a small bowl, mix the vegetable oil, turmeric, cumin, paprika, salt, black pepper, and garlic.
3. Rub the spice mixture all over the fish, making sure to get inside the cavity as well.
4. Place the fish on a large piece of aluminium foil and wrap it up tightly.
5. Place the foil-wrapped fish on the grill or in the oven and cook for 20-25 minutes, until the flesh is cooked through and flaky.
6. In a small bowl, mix the lemon juice, white vinegar, parsley, and cilantro.
7. Serve the Masgouf hot off the grill or out of the oven with the herb sauce on the side, along with Iraqi flatbread and pickled vegetables.

Enjoy the delicious and authentic flavours of Iraqi Masgouf!

Madgooga

SERVES

4

METHOD

POT

TIME

1 hour 20 mins

DIFFICULTY

4/10

Madgooga offers a unique combination of spices and textures, making it a flavorful and aromatic dessert that reflects the rich culinary traditions of Iraq. Enjoy this sweet cake as a delightful treat during gatherings or as a special indulgence.

1. Preheat your oven to 350°F (175°C). Grease and flour a cake pan.
2. In a large bowl, combine semolina, flour, sugar, baking powder, baking soda, salt, ground cardamom, and ground cinnamon.
3. Add yogurt and vegetable oil to the dry ingredients. Mix until well combined.
4. Fold in raisins and chopped nuts if using.
5. Pour the batter into the prepared cake pan and smooth the top.
6. Bake in the preheated oven for about 30-35 minutes or until a toothpick inserted into the centre comes out clean.

While the cake is baking, prepare the syrup.
1. In a saucepan, combine sugar, water, and lemon juice. Bring to a boil, then reduce the heat and simmer for about 10 minutes, or until the syrup slightly thickens.
2. Add rose water or orange blossom water if using.

Soak the Cake: Once the cake is out of the oven, immediately pour the hot syrup over it. Allow the cake to absorb the syrup and cool in the pan.
Once cooled, cut into squares or diamonds, and serve.
Madgooga is often enjoyed with a drizzle of additional syrup if desired.

INGREDIENTS:
For the Cake:
2 cups semolina
1 cup all-purpose flour
1 cup sugar
1 cup plain yogurt
1 cup vegetable oil
1 tsp baking powder
1/2 tsp baking soda
1/4 tsp salt
1 tsp ground cardamom
1 tsp ground cinnamon
1/2 cup raisins (optional)
1/2 cup chopped nuts (such as almonds or walnuts, optional)

For the Syrup:
1 cup sugar
1/2 cup water
1 tbsp lemon juice
1 tsp rose water or orange blossom water (optional)

Gobekli Tepe

Welcome to the delicious and vibrant world of ancient Turkish cuisine! It's one of the most diverse. This menu has been shaped by centuries of history, with influences from the Ottoman Empire, the Mediterranean, and the Middle East. It's all mixed up... but before it got mixed up, it was, and is, the most ancient civilisation we know of. Gobekli Tepe predates everything we know by thousands of years. Even the Pyramids.

What were they eating back then? In that crucial time between humans being hunter-gatherers... and us becoming farmers? Lamb and beef were the first to be farmed and the most commonly consumed. Eggplants, peppers, and cucumbers were all popular ingredients, often featured in dishes such as Imam Bayildi (stuffed eggplants) and dolma (stuffed vegetables).

Kebabs, meat stews, and meatballs were all popular dishes, often served with a side of rice or bulgur.
Turkish cuisine is also renowned for its use of spices and herbs. Cumin, sumac, and mint are all commonly used, as well as cinnamon, cardamom, and saffron giving them a unique flavour profile.

Another key feature of ancient Turkish cuisine is its love of sweets and desserts. Baklava, a pastry made of layers of phyllo dough and honey-soaked nuts, is perhaps the most famous of all Turkish desserts. Other sweet treats include Turkish delight, halva, and lokum.
Sweet or savoury, hearty stews to flavourful kebabs... People like good stuff... No matter when they live. Dig in... We all have good taste buds. We always have.

Did you know...
Shamanistic Beliefs: Before the arrival of Islam, the ancient Turks practised a form of shamanism. Shamans were believed to act as intermediaries between the physical and spiritual worlds, communicating with spirits and performing healing rituals. Shamanistic traditions continued to influence Turkish culture even after conversion to Islam.

SERVES
2

METHOD
PAN

TIME
15 mins

DIFFICULTY
4/10

INGREDIENTS:

1 cup plain flour
2 large eggs
1 cup milk
1/4 cup seaweed (wakame or nori) rehydrated and finely chopped
1/4 cup crumbled goat cheese
Salt and black pepper to taste
2 tbsp butter for cooking

For Serving (Optional):
1/2 cup plain yogurt
1 clove garlic
parsley, dill or mint
Pomegranate seeds for garnish

This recipe combines creamy goat cheese with briny seaweed, creating a delicious and light egg dish. The seaweed adds umami depth and texture, while the goat cheese brings richness. Perfect for breakfast or a quick meal, this Kaygana is both flavorful and healthy.

1. Reydrate the seaweed by soaking in warm water for 10 minutes, then drain and finely chop.
2. In a bowl, whisk eggs, flour, milk, salt and pepper until smooth. Fold in the seaweed and fresh herbs.
3. Add the crumbled goat cheese. Mix well.
4. Heat butter in a skillet over medium heat. Pour a thin layer of the mixture into the skillet, spreading it evenly. Allow the Kaygana to cook until the edges start to set.
5. Once the bottom is golden brown and the top is mostly set, you can either flip it like a pancake or fold it over, creating a Taco-like shape.
Cook until both sides are golden brown, and the goat cheese is melted.

Serve:
Cut the Kaygana into wedges and serve .
Optionally, mix yogurt, crushed garlic and herbs into a dip. garnish with pomegranate seeds for a unique twist.

Quote...
"The discovery of Göbekli Tepe is a thrilling reminder that there's still so much we don't know about our past. It ignites our curiosity and compels us to keep searching for answers about the origins of human civilization."
- Yuval Noah Harari

SERVES

4

METHOD

OVEN

TIME

45 mins

DIFFICULTY

5/10

A handheld explosion of flavour and textures. The magic lies in phyllo dough. Paper-thin layers, brushed with oil or butter, create a light, shatteringly crisp exterior. But Börek's true beauty lies in its adaptability. The filling is your canvas – crave cheese, vegetarian delights, or hearty meat? Surprisingly easy to make at home, Börek has stood the test of time for a reason.

1. Preheat the oven to 375°F. In a large skillet, heat the olive oil over medium-high heat. Add the ground meat and cook until browned, about 5-7 minutes.
2. Add the chopped onion and minced garlic to the skillet and sauté until softened, about 2-3 minutes.
3. Stir in the chopped parsley and mint, and season with salt and pepper.
4. Unroll the phyllo pastry dough and lay out on a clean surface. Brush each sheet with melted butter.
5. Spread the meat mixture over the phyllo pastry, leaving a small border around the edges. Sprinkle the crumbled feta cheese over the top.
6. Roll up the pastry dough into a log and tuck the ends under to form a crescent shape. Brush the top with more melted butter.
7. Place the borek on a baking sheet and bake in the oven for 30-35 minutes, or until golden brown and crispy.
8. Allow the borek to cool slightly before slicing and serving.

INGREDIENTS:

450g (1lb) ground lamb or beef
1 onion, chopped
2 cloves garlic, minced
2 tbsp olive oil
1/4 cup chopped fresh parsley
1/4 cup chopped fresh mint
Salt and pepper, to taste
1 package phyllo pastry dough
1/2 cup unsalted butter, melted
1 cup crumbled feta cheese

Would you rather...
Be the smartest person in your society (astronomy, mathematics, writing etc) and have no friends, Or be a very popular sheep herder?

SERVES
4

METHOD
PAN

TIME
90mins

DIFFICULTY
5/10

INGREDIENTS:

8-10 large vine leaves
2 tbsp Olive oil
1 onion, finely chopped
1/2 cup long-grain rice
1/4 cup currants

1/4 cup pine nuts
1 tsp Ground cinnamon
1tsp ground allspice
Salt and pepper, to taste
1 cup vegetable or chicken broth
1 lemon, juiced

Turkish Dolma stands out for its variety and delicate flavours. The use of grape leaves, a unique and elegant vessel, adds a touch of freshness. Plus, Dolma's versatility allows exploration with different vegetables and fillings, making it a fun and interactive dish for sharing.

1. Preheat the oven to 350°F (175°C).
2. Blanch the vine leaves in boiling water for 3-5 minutes, then drain and set aside.
3. In a large saucepan, heat the olive oil over medium heat.
4. Add the chopped onion and sauté until translucent.
5. Add the long-grain rice, currants, pine nuts, cinnamon, allspice, salt,
and pepper to the saucepan and stir until well combined.
6. Remove the saucepan from the heat and stir in 1/4 cup of the vegetable or chicken broth.
7. To assemble the Dolma, place a blanched vine leaf on a flat surface
and spoon about 1 tbsp. of the rice mixture onto the center of the leaf.
8. Fold the sides of the leaf inwards and roll it up tightly like a burrito.
9. Repeat with the remaining vine leaves and rice mixture.
10. Arrange the stuffed vine leaves in a baking dish and pour the remaining vegetable or chicken broth over the top.
11. Cover the baking dish with foil and bake the Dolma in the preheated oven for 30-40 minutes, or until the rice is cooked and the vegetables are tender.
12. Remove the foil from the baking dish and drizzle the Dolma with lemon juice.

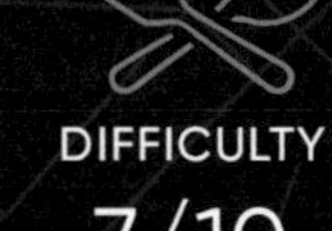

SERVES	METHOD	TIME	DIFFICULTY
12	OVEN	2 hours 15 mins	7/10

Golden phyllo layers, each buttery flake shattering to reveal a treasure trove of finely ground pistachios mingles with the warm sweetness of honey. If you haven't had Baklava before, you'll soon understand why it's survived so long. Delicious.

1. Preheat the oven to 350°F.
2. Mix together the chopped nuts and granulated sugar.
3. Brush a 9x13 inch baking dish with melted butter.
4. Lay a sheet of phyllo in the dish and brush with butter.
5. Repeat this process, layering 8-10 sheets of phyllo.
6. Sprinkle a layer of the nut mixture over the phyllo dough.
7. Add another layer of phyllo and brush with butter.
8. Repeat this process until you have used up all of the nut mixture.
9. Top the final layer of nuts with 8-10 more sheets of phyllo brushing each layer with butter.
10. Cut the baklava into small diamond shaped pieces.
11. Bake in the preheated oven for 30-40 minutes.
12. While the baklava is baking, make the syrup combining the water, honey, rose water, and lemon juice in a small saucepan.
13. Bring the syrup to a boil and then reduce heat to low and simmer for 10-15 minutes, or until the syrup has thickened.
14. Remove the baklava from the oven and immediately pour the syrup over the top of the pastry.
15. Allow the baklava to cool and absorb the syrup for at least 1 hour before serving. Enjoy!

INGREDIENTS:

1 lb phyllo dough

1 cup unsalted butter, melted

1, 1/2cups chopped mixed nuts (pistachios, walnuts, and almonds)

1/2 cup granulated sugar

1/2 cup water

1/4 cup honey

2 tbsp rose water

1 tbsp lemon juice

Modern Turkey

In ancient times, Turkish cuisine was heavily influenced by nomadic and pastoral lifestyles. Meat, particularly lamb and beef, was a staple of the diet, along with grains such as barley, wheat, and rice. Spices such as cumin, coriander, and mint were also used to add flavour.

Over time, Turkish cuisine has been influenced by various cultures, including Persian, Arab, Greek, and Ottoman. These influences have led to the introduction of new ingredients and cooking techniques. In modern times, Turkish cuisine is a unique blend of traditional flavours and modern influences. Popular dishes include kebabs, stuffed vegetables such as dolma, and hearty stews such as lentil soup. The use of spices such as paprika, sumac, and oregano add depth and complexity to many dishes.

One of the unique aspects of Turkish cuisine is the use of yogurt, which is used in dishes such as cacik, a refreshing cucumber and yogurt dip, and ayran, a yogurt drink.

Despite modern influences, Turkish cuisine still holds on to its traditional roots, as most do. Many families continue to use family recipes that have been passed down to them, and food plays an important role in Turkish culture. Europe and the Middle East became a crucible of cross-cultural flavours over time. But, overall, modern Turkish cuisine retained its individuality, even as it grew into what it is today. Turkish food is great.

DID YOU KNOW...

Tea is more than just a beverage in Turkey; it's a social ritual. Turkish black tea (çay) is consumed throughout the day, from breakfast to after dinner. Sharing a glass of tea signifies hospitality, friendship, and a chance to connect. The brewing method involves a special double teapot, and the tea is traditionally served strong in small tulip-shaped glasses.

Kizarmis Yumurta

SERVES
1

METHOD
PAN

TIME
7mins

DIFFICULTY
1/10

INGREDIENTS:

2 large eggs

2 tbsp butter

thyme

paprika

Salt and pepper to taste

Optional: Turkish bread, sliced tomatoes, sliced cucumbers, olives, and cheese for serving

Imagine a plate adorned with perfectly par-boiled eggs... that are also fried! Nestled beneath them lies a vibrant bed of softened, caramelized vegetables – juicy tomatoes, onions, and peppers, all bathed in olive oil. A sprinkle of fresh parsley adds a burst of freshness, while a squeeze of lemon ties it all together. Each bite is a delightful interplay of textures – the soft creaminess of the egg yolk, the satisfying chew of the vegetables, and pops of bright acidity from the lemon.

1. Boil your eggs, shell them and cut them in half
2. Heat the butter in a non-stick frying pan over medium-high heat.
3. Place eggs into the pan, cut side down, and sprinkle with thyme, paprika, salt and pepper.
4. Let the eggs cook until the edges are crispy and golden brown, about 2-3 minutes.
5. Use a spatula to carefully transfer the eggs to a plate.
6. Serve with Turkish bread, sliced tomatoes, sliced cucumbers, olives, and cheese if desired.

Enjoy your delicious Turkish Kizarmis Yumurta for breakfast!

QUOTE...
"If one had but a single glance to give the world,
one should gaze on Istanbul."
- Alphonse de Lamartine

KUMPIR

SERVES
4

METHOD
POT

TIME
75 mins

DIFFICULTY
5/10

Travel to Istanbul and discover Kumpir, a giant potato extravaganza. This isn't your average loaded spud – it's a choose-your-own-adventure flavour bomb!
A massive baked potato, crisp on the outside and fluffy within. Kumpir's beauty lies in its customization. It's a blank canvas for your cravings! Whether you crave classic combinations or adventurous mixes, Kumpir lets you be the chef. Vendors often have a mind-boggling array of toppings, making it a fun and interactive experience.

1. Preheat your oven to 375°F.
2. Scrub the potatoes well and prick them all over with a fork. Place the potatoes on a baking sheet and bake them in the preheated oven for about an hour, or until they are tender and can be easily pierced with a fork.
3. Cut a small slit in the top of each potato and gently squeeze them to open them up. Use a fork to lightly mash the insides of the potatoes.
4. Add a dollop of butter, a spoonful of sour cream, and a handful of shredded cheddar cheese to each potato. Season with salt and black pepper to taste.
5. Add your desired toppings to each potato. This can include chopped green onions, sliced black olives, pickled red cabbage, pickled cucumbers, and chopped fresh parsley.
6. Serve hot and enjoy your delicious Turkish Kumpir! over the dumplings and serve hot.

INGREDIENTS:

4 large baking potatoes
1 cup shredded cheddar cheese
1/2 cup butter, softened
1/2 cup sour cream
1/2 cup chopped green onions
1/2 cup sliced black olives
1/2 cup pickled red cabbage
1/2 cup pickled cucumbers
1/2 cup chopped fresh parsley
Salt and black pepper, to taste

WOULD YOU RATHER...
A balloon ride in Cappadocia or a concert in the Basilica Cisterns?

MANTI

SERVES
4

METHOD
POT

TIME
75 mins

DIFFICULTY
5/10

INGREDIENTS:

For the Dough:
2 cups all-purpose flour
1 egg
1/2 cup warm water
1 tsp salt

For the Filling:
250g (1/2lb) ground beef or lamb
1 small onion, finely chopped
1/2 tsp salt
1/4 tsp black pepper
1/4 tsp ground cinnamon
1/4 tsp ground allspice

For the Sauce:
1 cup plain yogurt
1 clove garlic, minced
1 tbsp melted butter
1 tbsp dried mint
1/4 tsp cayenne pepper
Salt to taste

Manti, delectable little dumplings bursting with flavour. Unlike their heavy cousins, pierogies, these bite-sized delights are a dance of textures and taste.
Manti's secret weapon? Size. Traditionally very small, they showcase the cook's skill and patience. Dumplings find fans worldwide, but Turkish Manti stand out for their size and unique cooking methods. Enjoy them simply with yogurt or tomato sauce, or add a kick with spicy chilli oil.

1. In a mixing bowl, combine the flour, egg, water, and salt. Mix well and
knead the dough until it's smooth and elastic. Cover the dough with a
damp towel and let it rest for 30 minutes.
2. In a separate bowl, combine the ground meat, onion, salt, black
pepper, cinnamon, and allspice. Mix well until fully combined.
3. On a floured surface, roll out the dough to a thin sheet. Cut out small
circles of dough using a cookie cutter or glass. Spoon a small amount of the meat mixture onto each circle, and fold the dough over to form a small dumpling. Press the edges together to seal.
4. In a large pot of boiling water, cook the dumplings in batches until they rise to the surface, about 8-10 minutes. Remove with a slotted spoon and place in a serving dish.
5. To make the sauce, whisk together the yogurt, garlic, melted butter, dried mint, cayenne pepper, and salt. Pour the sauce over the dumplings and serve hot.

DONDURMA

SERVES	METHOD	TIME	DIFFICULTY
4	ICECREAM MAKER	4 hours	4/10

Dondurma is known for its delightful stretchiness and resistance to melting, creating a playful and memorable experience. The addition of salep and mastic gives it a unique flavour profile that sets Turkish ice cream apart.

1. In a small bowl, mix the salep powder with a small amount of the cold milk to create a smooth paste.
2. In a saucepan, combine the remaining milk, heavy cream, sugar, and a pinch of salt. Heat the mixture over medium heat, stirring occasionally until it reaches a simmer.
3. Gradually whisk in the salep mixture, continuing to stir to avoid lumps.
4. Add the crushed mastic gum and keep stirring until the mixture thickens to a custard-like consistency.
5. Allow the mixture to cool completely. Once cooled, pour it into an ice cream maker and churn according to the manufacturer's instructions until it reaches a thick, creamy consistency.
6. Dondurma is traditionally served with a unique stretchy and elastic texture. To achieve this, remove the churned ice cream from the machine, place it in a lidded container, and freeze for a few hours until firm.
7. Just before serving, knead and pull the ice cream vigorously using a spoon or paddle. This step is what gives Dondurma its distinctive chewiness.

Scoop the Dondurma into bowls or cones and enjoy the unique texture and flavours.

INGREDIENTS:

2 cups whole milk

1 cup heavy cream

1 cup sugar

2 tbsp salep powder (if unavailable, use cornstarch as a substitute)

1/2 tsp mastic gum, crushed into a powder

A pinch of salt

Ancient Sparta

Ancient Sparta. Heroes and Warriors. Discipline and sacrifice. While the Spartan diet was known for its simplicity and emphasis on functionality rather than flavour, there are still some interesting dishes and ingredients worth exploring.

One of the staples of Spartan cuisine was black broth, a soup made from boiled pork, vinegar, and blood. While it might not sound particularly appetising, it was considered a delicacy among the Spartans and was said to give them strength and endurance.

Another popular ingredient in Spartan cuisine was barley, which was used to make a variety of dishes such as porridge and bread. Barley was a staple in the Spartan diet due to its high nutritional value and ability to grow in harsh conditions.

Meat was also a part of the Spartan diet, with pork, lamb, and goat being the most commonly consumed. These meats were often grilled or roasted and served with simple seasonings such as salt and oregano. Vegetables were not as prominent in the Spartan diet, but they were still eaten. Onions and garlic were often used to add flavour to dishes, while beans and lentils were a source of protein.

Cheese was also an important part of Spartan cuisine, with feta being the most common type. Feta was often crumbled over dishes or served alongside bread and olives.

If you're looking to recreate some classic Spartan dishes in your kitchen, try making a simple barley porridge with honey and nuts for breakfast, or grilling some lamb chops with oregano and lemon juice for dinner. While Spartan cuisine may not be as elaborate as other ancient cuisines, its simplicity and focus on function make it a fascinating glimpse into the diet of ancient warriors.

Did you know...

Fear of Corruption: Iron Money: In a unique move to discourage materialism and corruption, Sparta used iron rods as currency. This bulky and cumbersome form of money made it difficult to hoard wealth and ensured a focus on a warrior's honour rather than personal riches.

SERVES

2

METHOD

PAN

TIME

30 mins

DIFFICULTY

4/10

INGREDIENTS:

For the Lentil and Herb Patties:
1 cup lentils, cooked
1/2 cup barley flour
1/4 cup fresh mint, finely chopped
1/4 cup fresh coriander, finely chopped
1/4 cup green onions, finely chopped
1 garlic clove, minced
Salt and black pepper to taste
Olive oil for cooking

For the Yogurt Drizzle:

1/2 cup Greek yogurt
1 tbsp olive oil
1 tsp honey
Zest of one lemon
Salt to taste

This inventive breakfast dish takes inspiration from Spartan simplicity, incorporating lentils, barley, and fresh herbs. The yogurt drizzle adds a creamy and tangy element, creating a unique and flavorful combination. While details about specific Spartan recipes are speculative, this creative interpretation aims to capture the essence of the Spartan spirit with a modern twist. Enjoy this unique and exotic Spartan-inspired breakfast!

Prepare Lentil and Herb Patties:
1. In a bowl, mash the cooked lentils. Add barley flour, chopped mint, chopped coriander, chopped green onions, minced garlic, salt, and black pepper. Mix well to form a dough.
2. Shape the mixture into small, flat patties
3. Heat olive oil in a pan over medium heat. Cook the lentil and herb patties until golden brown on both sides, ensuring they are cooked through.

Prepare Yogurt Drizzle:
4. In a separate bowl, whisk together Greek yogurt, olive oil, honey, lemon zest, and a pinch of salt. Adjust the sweetness and acidity to your liking.
5. Arrange the lentil and herb patties on a plate and drizzle the yogurt mixture over them.
6. Garnish with additional fresh herbs, pomegranate seeds, or a sprinkle of crushed nuts for added texture and flavor.

Quote…
"He who sweats more in training bleeds less in war."
-Spartan Ethos

Unlike elaborate stews, this dish celebrates simplicity, mirroring the Spartan spirit.

A robust concoction overflowing with melt-in-your-mouth lamb and chewy barley bathed in a richly savoury broth. Each mouthful transports you back in time, a taste of the fuel that sustained Sparta's legendary warriors.

1. In a large pot, heat the olive oil and add the diced lamb. Cook until browned on all sides.
2. Add the onion and garlic to the pot and cook until softened.
3. Add the diced carrot and celery and cook for a few minutes until slightly softened.
4. Add the barley and water to the pot and bring to a boil.
5. Reduce heat to a simmer and cover the pot. Cook for 1 to 1.5 hours, or until the lamb and barley are tender.
6. Season with salt and pepper to taste.

Serve the lamb and barley stew hot for a hearty and nutritious Spartan lunch.

INGREDIENTS:

450g (1lb) of lamb, diced

1 cup of barley

4 cups of water

1 onion, diced

2 garlic cloves, minced

1 carrot, diced

1 celery stalk, diced

2 tbsp of olive oil

Salt and pepper to taste

Would you rather…
Be raised as a student of Socrates or as a Spartan warrior?

INGREDIENTS:

450g (1lb) boneless pork shoulder, cut into bite-sized pieces

1 cup fresh pig blood (or substitute with 1/2 cup cooked, crumbled blood sausage)

4 cups water

1/2 cup red wine vinegar

1 onion, chopped

2 bay leaves

1 tbsp salt
Black pepper to taste

Spartan Black Broth. Unlike creamy soups, this is a bold, intense experience for your taste buds. The color might be unexpected but trust the journey. Pork and its blood simmer for hours, creating a rich, deeply savoury broth. A splash of vinegar cuts through the intensity, while salt adds balance. Every spoonful is a taste of history – the fuel of Spartan warriors, renowned for their strength.

1. In a large pot, bring the water to a boil. Add the pork and bay leaves. Reduce heat and simmer for 45 minutes to 1 hour, or until the pork is tender.
2. While the pork simmers, if using fresh blood, whisk it in a separate bowl with a little water to prevent clumping.
3. Once the pork is cooked, remove it from the pot with a slotted spoon and set aside. Reserve about 1 cup of the cooking liquid.
4. Increase heat to medium and add the vinegar to the remaining broth in the pot. Scrape up any browned bits from the bottom.
5. Slowly whisk in the reserved cooking liquid back into the pot.
6. If using fresh blood, slowly whisk it into the pot and bring to a simmer. If using blood sausage, crumble it into the pot and simmer for a few minutes to combine flavors.
7. Add the chopped onion and simmer for an additional 5 minutes, or until the onion is softened.
8. Season with salt and black pepper to taste.
9. Return the cooked pork to the pot and heat through for a few minutes.
10. Serve hot.

SERVES

5

METHOD

OVEN

TIME

30 mins

DIFFICULTY

3/10

Spartan Honey & Walnut Phyllo Rolls offer a delicate twist on classic desserts. Unlike dense pastries, these are crispy, flaky bites bursting with flavour.

Golden phyllo, a warm, gooey centre, toasted walnuts bathed in fragrant honey syrup. This dessert combines the sweetness of honey with the crunch of walnuts, and is sure to satisfy any sweet tooth.

1. Preheat oven to 350°F.
2. In a small bowl, mix together the walnuts, honey, and spices.
3. Lay out a sheet of phyllo dough and brush it with melted butter.
4. Add a spoonful of the walnut mixture onto the bottom of the phyllo sheet.
5. Roll the sheet up tightly, folding in the sides as you go.
6. Repeat with remaining phyllo sheets and filling.
7. Brush the tops of the rolls with more melted butter.
8. Bake for 15-20 minutes, until golden brown.
9. Allow to cool slightly before dusting with powdered sugar.

INGREDIENTS:

1/2 cup walnuts, finely chopped

1/4 cup honey

1/2 tsp ground cinnamon

4 tsp ground cloves

8 sheets phyllo dough

1/4 cup butter, melted

Powdered sugar for garnish

Modern Greece

Over time, Greek cuisine has been influenced by various cultures, including Roman, Byzantine, Ottoman, and Venetian. These influences have led to the introduction of new ingredients and cooking techniques, as well as changes in dietary restrictions.

But overall, as with all others, Greek cuisine is a unique blend of traditional flavours and modern influences. Popular dishes include moussaka, a layered dish with eggplant and ground meat, and souvlaki, grilled meat skewers served with pita bread and tzatziki sauce. The use of spices such as cinnamon, cumin, and allspice add depth and complexity to many dishes.

One of the unique aspects of Greek cuisine is the use of feta cheese, which is used in dishes such as spanakopita, a spinach and feta pie, and Greek salad. Olives and olive oil are also a hallmark of Greek cuisine and are used in dishes such as dolmades, stuffed grape leaves filled with rice and herbs.v The Greeks love their olives and they love their seafood. And while recipes change, some ingredients stay the same. Some flavours are just great and never leave us.

Overall, Greek cuisine is a delightful mix of ancient and modern flavours, with unique dishes and spices that set it apart from other cuisines. Lemon, olives, seafood and meat, Greek recipes include some of the tastiest ingredients there are... enjoy

DID YOU KNOW...
The Name Game: Greece isn't actually called "Greece" by its inhabitants. In Modern Greek, the country is called "Hellas" (Ελλάς), a reference to the Hellenes, an ancient Greek tribe. "Greece" is the English name derived from the Latin word "Graecia."

Alevropita

SERVES
6

METHOD
OVEN

TIME
2 hours

DIFFICULTY
5/10

INGREDIENTS:

450g (1lb) phyllo dough sheets

1/2 cup olive oil

1/2 cup water

1/2 cup all-purpose flour

450g (1lb) spinach, washed and chopped

220g (1/2lb) feta cheese, crumbled

1 onion, chopped

2 cloves garlic, minced

2 eggs

Salt and pepper to taste

Alevropita is a crispy feta pie. So good. A rustic, one-pan wonder that's bursting with flavour. Imagine a thin, crispy crust cradling a creamy, cheesy centre. Alevropita, which literally translates to "flour pie," lets the quality ingredients speak for themselves.

1. Preheat the oven to 375°F (190°C).
2. In a large bowl, mix the spinach, feta cheese, onion, garlic, eggs, salt, and pepper.
3. In a small bowl, mix the olive oil and water.
4. Brush a baking dish with some of the olive oil mixture.
5. Lay a sheet of phyllo dough on the bottom of the dish and brush it with the olive oil mixture. Repeat with another sheet of phyllo, brushing it with the olive oil mixture.
6. Sprinkle some of the flour over the phyllo sheets.
7. Add a layer of the spinach mixture on top of the phyllo.
8. Repeat steps 5-7 until all the spinach mixture is used.
9. Finish with a layer of phyllo on top, brushing each sheet with the olive oil mixture.
10. Brush the top layer of phyllo with the remaining olive oil mixture.
11. Score the top layer of phyllo into squares or diamond shapes.
12. Bake in the preheated oven for about 45-50 minutes or until the top is golden brown and crispy.
13. Remove from the oven and let cool for a few minutes before slicing and serving.

Quote...
"It takes a lifetime to discover Greece, but it only takes an instant to fall in love with her."
-Henry Miller

GEMISTO XIFIA

SERVES
4

METHOD
OVEN

TIME
30mins

DIFFICULTY
3/10

The Greeks love their seafood. And most of the time there's no recipe needed. prawns, lobster, oysters, octopus... a lot of the time these things just need a bit of fire... a wedge of lemon, and they're good to go... But here's a dish I love. Stuffed Swordfish.
Imagine a hot summer evening, the scent of grilling fish wafting through the air, and a plate piled high with vibrant flavours. Tonight, we're diving into Greek Stuffed Swordfish with Feta and Olives This recipe is a fusion of textures and tastes that will transport you to the heart of the Mediterranean.

1. Preheat oven to 375°F.
2. In a mixing bowl, combine the spinach, feta cheese, Kalamata olives, parsley, dill, oregano, thyme, lemon zest, and 2 tablespoons of the
olive oil. Mix well.
3. Cut a pocket into the side of each swordfish steak, being careful not to cut all the way through.
4. Stuff the spinach and feta mixture into the pocket of each swordfish steak.
5. Brush the remaining olive oil over the swordfish steaks and season with salt and pepper.
6. Heat a large oven-safe skillet over medium-high heat. When the skillet is hot, add the swordfish steaks and sear for 2-3 minutes on each side until browned.
7. Transfer the skillet to the oven and bake for 10-12 minutes or until the swordfish is cooked through and flakes easily with a fork.
8. Serve hot and enjoy!

INGREDIENTS:

4 swordfish steaks, 170g (6oz) each
1/2 cup chopped spinach
1/2 cup crumbled feta cheese
1/4 cup chopped Kalamata olives
2 tbsp chopped fresh parsley
2 tbsp chopped fresh dill
1 tbsp chopped fresh oregano
1 tbsp chopped fresh thyme
1 tbsp lemon zest
1/4 cup olive oil
Salt and pepper

WOULD YOU RATHER...

Spend a week on the Greek Island of your choice with unlimited money, but be unable to leave... or spend a month travelling wherever you want with $2000 a week

Kotopoulo Souvlaki

SERVES
4

METHOD
GRILL

TIME
45 mins

DIFFICULTY
2/10

INGREDIENTS:

4 boneless, skinless chicken breasts
2 tbsp olive oil
2 tbsp lemon juice
2 tbsp Greek yogurt
1 tbsp dried oregano
1 tsp dried thyme
1 tsp paprika
1/2 tsp garlic powder
1/2 tsp onion powder
Salt and pepper, to taste
1 red onion, cut into wedges
1 red bell pepper, cut into chunks
1 green bell pepper, cut into chunks
1 zucchini, sliced into rounds
Wooden or metal skewers

Who doesn't like a Kebab after a couple of drinks? If you're in Greece you've probably had a couple in the afternoon sun. Now you don't even have to go to the kebab shop! You can make them at home. You're welcome. Tender, juicy, marinated chicken pieces that char slightly on the grill, mingling with crisp bell peppers, red onions, and all the flavours of the Mediterranean. What's not to like?

1. Cut the chicken breasts into 1-inch cubes and place them in a large bowl.
2. In a small bowl, whisk together the olive oil, lemon juice, Greek yogurt, oregano, thyme, paprika, garlic powder, onion powder, salt, and pepper.
3. Pour the marinade over the chicken and toss to coat. Cover and refrigerate for at least 30 minutes or up to 4 hours.
4. When ready to grill, preheat your grill to medium-high heat. If using wooden skewers, soak them in water for at least 30 minutes before grilling.
5. Thread the marinated chicken, onion wedges, bell pepper chunks, and zucchini slices onto the skewers, alternating the ingredients as you go.
6. Grill the kebabs for 10-12 minutes, turning occasionally, until the chicken is cooked through and the vegetables are tender and lightly charred.
7. Remove the kebabs from the grill and let them rest for a few minutes before serving.
8. Serve hot with a side of tzatziki sauce or Greek salad, if desired. Enjoy.

Loukoumades

SERVES	METHOD	TIME	DIFFICULTY
2	POT	2hours 15mins	3/10

Tonight, we're celebrating a taste of Greece with Loukoumades, those adorable little puffs of golden perfection. A unique and delightful modern Greek dessert, Loukoumades are small, deep-fried dough balls, similar to doughnut holes, drizzled with honey or syrup and sprinkled with various toppings.

Prepare the Dough:
1. In a bowl, dissolve the sugar in lukewarm water.
2. Sprinkle the yeast over the water and let it sit for 5-10 minutes until it becomes frothy.
3. In a large mixing bowl, combine the flour and salt. Pour in the yeast mixture and mix until a smooth batter forms.
4. Cover the bowl with a kitchen towel and let the dough rise for 1-2 hours, or until it has doubled in size.

Fry the Loukoumades:
5. Heat vegetable oil in a deep fryer or a heavy-bottomed pot to 350°F (175°C).
6. Using two spoons, drop small portions of the dough into the hot oil. Fry until golden brown, turning them to ensure even cooking.
7. Remove with a slotted spoon and drain on paper towels.

Drizzle with Honey and Add Toppings:
8. While the loukoumades are still warm, drizzle them generously with honey.
9. Sprinkle chopped nuts (such as walnuts or pistachios) over the honey-coated loukoumades.

Optionally, add a dash of cinnamon or sesame seeds for extra flavour.

INGREDIENTS:

For the Dough:
2 cups all-purpose flour
1 tsp active dry yeast
1 cup lukewarm water
1/2 tsp salt
1 tsp sugar

For Frying:
Vegetable oil for deep frying

For Topping:
Honey
Chopped nuts (such as walnuts or pistachios)
Cinnamon (optional)
Sesame seeds (optional)

ANCIENT PERSIA

Welcome to the exotic and flavourful world of ancient Persian cuisine! Persian cuisine has a rich and varied history, with influences from the Middle East, Central Asia, and the Mediterranean.
One of the hallmarks of Persian cuisine is its use of fresh herbs, which are used to add depth and complexity to dishes. Mint, parsley, and cilantro are all commonly used, as well as dill, tarragon, and saffron. These herbs are often combined with fruits, nuts, and meats to create a wide range of dishes.

Meat is an important part of Persian cuisine, with lamb and beef being the most commonly used. Kebabs, meat stews, and meatballs are all popular dishes, often served with rice or flatbread.
Rice is a staple in Persian cuisine, and it is often flavoured with saffron and other spices. Rice dishes such as polo and chelow are served with a variety of accompaniments, including vegetables, meats, and dried fruits.
Another key ingredient in Persian cuisine is pomegranate, which is used to add a tart and fruity flavour to dishes. Pomegranate molasses is often used in marinades and dressings, while the seeds are sprinkled over salads and desserts.

Persian cuisine is also known for its sweet and savoury stews, which are often made with a combination of fruits, nuts, and meats. One popular dish is fesenjan, a stew made with chicken or duck, pomegranate molasses, and ground walnuts.
If you want to explore the rich and varied flavours of ancient Persian cuisine, why not try your hand at some classic dishes? Some popular dishes include kebab koobideh, a grilled meat skewer, and ash-e-reshteh, a hearty soup made with beans, noodles, and herbs.
So come and discover the exotic and delicious flavours of ancient Persian cuisine. Whether you're looking for bold and spicy flavours or sweet and fruity desserts, Persian cuisine is sure to delight your taste buds and transport you to a land of history and culture.

Did you know...
Champions of Religious Tolerance: The Achaemenid Empire, which ruled much of the ancient world from the 6th to 4th centuries BCE, was surprisingly tolerant of conquered peoples' religions. Unlike some empires that sought to impose their beliefs, the Persians allowed conquered populations to freely practice their own faiths. This tolerance helped to maintain stability and peace within the vast empire.

ROSEWATER & SAFFRON PANCAKES

SERVES
4

METHOD
PAN

TIME
50 mins

DIFFICULTY
5/10

INGREDIENTS:

For the Pancakes:
1 cup rice flour
1 cup almond flour
1 tsp ground cardamom
1/2 tsp ground saffron threads (steeped in 2 tbsp warm water)
2 tbsp rosewater
1 cup almond milk (or any nut milk)
2 tbsp melted ghee or clarified butter
Pinch of salt
Ghee or oil for cooking

Syrup:
1/2 cup shelled pistachios, finely chopped
1/2 cup dates, pitted and finely chopped
1/2 cup water
1 tbsp rosewater
1 tbsp orange blossom water (optional)
Crushed dried rose petals for garnish

Like the other cultures explored in this book, there's a significant contrast in the cuisine enjoyed by the wealthier and poorer classes. The Ancient Persians were no exception. Here's a more refined recipe representing a breakfast favoured by the affluent class.

Prepare the Pistachio Date Syrup:
1. In a saucepan, combine chopped pistachios, chopped dates, and water. Simmer over low heat until the mixture thickens into a syrup-like consistency.
2. Stir in rosewater and orange blossom water (if using). Set aside to cool.
3. In a bowl, combine rice flour, almond flour, ground cardamom, saffron-infused water, rosewater, almond milk, melted ghee or clarified butter, and a pinch of salt. Mix until you have a smooth batter.
4. Heat ghee or oil in a skillet over medium heat. Pour a ladleful of batter onto the skillet to form a pancake.
5. Cook until bubbles form on the surface, then flip and cook the other side until golden brown.
Repeat until all the batter is used.
6. Stack the saffron and rosewater pancakes on a plate. Drizzle generously with the pistachio date syrup.
7. Garnish with crushed dried rose petals for an extra touch of Persian elegance.

Embrace the unique flavours of ancient Persia with these fragrant and exotic pancakes. Serve alongside a cup of Persian tea for an authentic experience.

Quote...
"Be happy for this moment. This moment is your life."
-Omah Khayyam

SERVES
2

METHOD
GRILL

TIME
3 hours

DIFFICULTY
4/10

Tonight, we're taking a trip to Persia with Kabab Barg, a succulent, melt-in-your-mouth experience unlike any grilled meat you've had before. This is all about juicy perfection. Imagine tender strips of marinated beef or lamb, bursting with flavour in every bite. The secret lies in the marinade, a blend of incredible fresh ingredients.

Ancient Persian cuisine was known for its lavish use of spices, herbs, and fruits. But this dish shows that they also practised estraint, allowing great flavours to shine on their own. Here is a recipe for a fancy Persian lunch:

1. In a bowl, combine the grated onion, olive oil, lemon juice, saffron, salt, and pepper.
2. Add the sliced beef to the bowl and mix well to coat the meat in the marinade.
3. Cover the bowl and let the meat marinate in the refrigerator for at least 2 hours, or overnight.
4. Preheat a grill or broiler to high heat.
5. Thread the beef slices onto skewers and grill or broil for 3-4 minutes on each side, or until cooked to your desired level of doneness.
6. Serve the Kebab-e Barg hot with steamed basmati rice and a side of grilled vegetables or salad.

Enjoy this delicious and flavourful Persian lunch, fit for a king!

INGREDIENTS:

450g (1lb) of beef sirloin, thinly sliced

1 onion, grated

1/4 cup of olive oil

2 tbsp of lemon juice

1 tsp of saffron

Salt and pepper to taste

Crushed dried rose petals for garnish (optional)

Would you rather...
Be a Persian Rug weaver or be the gardener responsible for the elaborate Royal Pasargadae Gardens

SERVES

4

METHOD

POT

TIME

1hour 30mins

DIFFICULTY

3/10

INGREDIENTS:

1 whole chicken, cut into serving pieces
2 cups finely ground walnuts
2 cups pomegranate molasses
1 large onion, finely chopped
3 tbsp vegetable oil
1 tsp ground cinnamon
1/2 tsp ground turmeric
Salt and pepper to taste
1 tbsp sugar (optional, to balance the tartness)
Pomegranate seeds for garnish (optional)

This Persian Pomegranate Stew is a savoury and sumptuous dish that combines the richness of ground walnuts, the tartness of pomegranate molasses, and tender pieces of meat, often chicken or duck. The result is a velvety, complex stew, balancing sweet and sour flavours, and symbolizing the culinary artistry of Persian cuisine. Unique and delicious.

1. In a food processor, grind the walnuts until they form a smooth paste. Be careful not to over-process, as you don't want it to turn into nut butter.
2. In a large pot, heat the vegetable oil over medium heat. Add the chopped onion and sauté until golden brown.
3. Add the chicken pieces and brown them on all sides.
4. Sprinkle ground cinnamon, ground turmeric, salt, and pepper over the chicken, stirring to coat evenly.
5. Stir in the ground walnuts, followed by the pomegranate molasses. Mix well to combine. If the stew is too thick, you can add a bit of water to achieve your desired consistency.
7. Reduce the heat to low, cover the pot, and let the stew simmer for 1.5 to 2 hours. Make sure the chicken is cooked through and tender.
8. Taste and adjust the seasoning. If it's too tart, you can add a tablespoon of sugar to balance the flavours.
9. Serve the Persian Pomegranate Stew over rice or with flatbread.

Optionally, garnish with pomegranate seeds for a burst of freshness and additional visual appeal.

SERVES
4

METHOD
PAN

TIME
35 mins

DIFFICULTY
5/10

Persian Halva is unique in its simplicity and focuses on those beautiful roasted nutty flavours. It's a textural adventure too – a bit crumbly at first, then giving way to a rich, satisfying melt. It's perfect for an after-dinner treat alongside a cup of strong coffee or steeped tea. So, skip the ordinary and dive into the captivating world of Persian Halva. You won't regret it!

INGREDIENTS:

1 cup sesame seeds

1 cup sugar

1/2 cup water

1/2 cup chopped pistachios or almonds (optional)

1. Toast the sesame seeds in a dry skillet over medium heat until they are lightly golden and fragrant, about 5-7 minutes. Be careful not to burn them.
2. In a separate saucepan, combine the sugar and water and bring to a boil. Reduce the heat and simmer until the sugar has dissolved and the mixture has thickened slightly, about 5-7 minutes.
3. Add the toasted sesame seeds to the sugar syrup and stir well to combine. Cook over medium heat, stirring constantly, until the mixture thickens and starts to pull away from the sides of the pan, about 15-20 minutes.
4. Remove from heat and stir in the chopped nuts, if using.
5. Pour the mixture into a greased dish and smooth the top with a spatula. Allow to cool completely before slicing into squares or diamonds.

Halva can be enjoyed on its own as a sweet treat or served with tea or coffee as a snack. It's a great way to end a meal on a sweet note!

MODERN IRAN

In modern times, Iranian cuisine is a unique blend of traditional flavours and modern influences. Popular dishes include kebabs, stews such as ghormeh sabzi, and rice dishes such as tahchin. The use of herbs such as parsley, mint, and dill add freshness and flavour to many dishes.

One of the unique aspects of Iranian cuisine is the use of dried fruits such as raisins, apricots, and dates, which are used in dishes such as jewelled rice and stews. Pomegranate, another staple of Iranian cuisine, is used to add tanginess to many dishes, including the popular fesenjan stew.

Despite modern influences, Iranian cuisine still holds on to its traditional roots. Many families continue to use family recipes that have been passed down for generations, and food plays an important role in Iranian culture and hospitality. Overall, Iranian cuisine is a delightful mix of ancient and modern flavours, with unique dishes and spices that set it apart from other cuisines.

Whether you're a seasoned cook or a beginner, there's no shortage of delicious flavours to explore in Iranian cuisine. So gather your ingredients and get ready to experience the vibrant and flavourful world of Iranian cooking!

DID YOU KNOW...

The Weekend Switch: Friday is the official start of the weekend in Iran, unlike Saturday and Sunday in most Western countries. This allows families and friends to gather for social events and religious observance on Fridays, promoting a strong sense of community and shared traditions. Thursday evenings often have a festive atmosphere as people prepare for the weekend.

Iranian Dips

SERVES
6

METHOD
OVEN

TIME
2 hours

DIFFICULTY
5/10

INGREDIENTS:
Kashk-e-Bademjan (Eggplant and Whey Dip):
2 medium eggplants
1/2 cup whey (kashk) or sourcream
2 cloves garlic, minced
1/4 cup chopped fresh mint
Salt and pepper, to taste

Borani-e-Esfanaaj (Spinach and Yogurt Dip)
2 cups cooked spinach, chopped
2 cups plain Greek yogurt
1 clove garlic, minced
1 tbsp olive oil
Salt and pepper, to taste

Iranians love their dips... If you've got enough different dips, bread can be a meal! In fact most of the dips we think of when we think of dips come from this region. So lets dip in shall we: These are light, refreshing, and perfect for dipping warm flatbread.

For Kashk-e-Bademjan:
Preheat your oven to 400°F.
Prick the eggplants with a fork and place them on a baking sheet.
Roast in the oven for 45-50 minutes, or until they are soft and the skin is charred.
Remove the eggplants from the oven and let them cool.
Peel off the skin and discard.
In a mixing bowl, mash the eggplant with a fork or a potato masher.
Add the whey (or sour cream), garlic, mint, salt, and pepper.
Mix well and chill for at least 30 minutes before serving.

For Borani-e-Esfanaaj:
In a mixing bowl, mix together the cooked spinach, yogurt, garlic, olive oil, salt, and pepper.
Chill for at least 30 minutes before serving.

To serve, place the three dips in separate bowls and serve with pita bread, crackers, or fresh vegetables. Enjoy!

QUOTE...

"Every man is the smith of his own fortune."

-Iranian Proverb

TAHCHEEN-E MORGH

SERVES
4

METHOD
OVEN

TIME
1 hour 35mins

DIFFICULTY
4/10

1. Rinse the basmati rice several times in cold water until the water runs clear. Soak the rice in cold water for at least 2 hours.
2. In a mixing bowl, combine the chicken, yogurt, turmeric, salt, and pepper. Mix well and let marinate for at least 30 minutes.
3. In a large pot, sauté the chopped onions in vegetable oil over medium heat until they are golden brown. Remove the onions from the pot and set aside.
4. In the same pot, add the marinated chicken and cook for about 10 minutes, stirring occasionally, until the chicken is cooked through.
5. Dissolve the saffron in 1/4 cup of hot water.
6. In a separate pot, boil 8 cups of water with salt. Drain the soaked rice cook the rice for about 10 minutes, or until it is slightly undercooked. Drain the rice and set aside.
7. In a mixing bowl, whisk together the yogurt and saffron water.
8. Preheat the oven to 350°F.
9. In a large mixing bowl, combine the cooked rice, chicken, sautéed onions, and yogurt mixture. Mix well.
10. Melt the butter in the pot that was used to cook the onions.
11. Spread a layer of the rice mixture over the bottom of the pot. Add another layer of the rice mixture on top of the chicken, and repeat until all of the rice and chicken mixture is used up. Smooth the top layer.
12. Pour the melted butter over the top layer of the rice.
13. Cover the pot with a lid and place it in the preheated oven. Bake for 30-40 minutes, or until the rice is golden brown on top and crispy. Remove the pot from the oven and let it rest for 5-10 minutes before serving.
15. To serve, flip the pot upside down onto a large serving platter, so that the crispy rice layer is on top. Enjoy!

INGREDIENTS:

2 cups basmati rice
450g (1lb) boneless, skinless chicken breasts, cut into small cubes
2 onions, chopped
1 tsp turmeric
1/2 tsp ground saffron
1/2 cup plain Greek yogurt
1/2 cup vegetable oil
3 tbsp butter
Salt and pepper, to taste

For the chicken marinade:
1 cup plain Greek yogurt
1/2 tsp turmeric
Salt and pepper, to taste

WOULD YOU RATHER...
Spend a week in Nushabad underground city without coming outside, or spend a week in the desert with local Bakhtiari?

Khoresht-e Karafs

SERVES	METHOD	TIME	DIFFICULTY
4	PAN	1 hour 45mins	4/10

INGREDIENTS:

450g (1lb) beef or lamb, cubed
4 cups celery, chopped into 1-inch pieces
1 large onion, finely chopped
2 tbsp vegetable oil
1 cup fresh parsley, finely chopped
1 cup fresh mint, finely chopped
2 tbsp dried fenugreek leaves (shanbalileh), crushed
1 tsp ground turmeric
Salt and pepper to taste
1 tbsp tomato paste
1 cup water
1 tbsp lemon juice

Travel to the heart of Persia and dig into Khoresh-e Karafs, a vibrant stew brimming with fresh celery and fragrant herbs. Melt-in-your-mouth lamb, slow-cooked until tender, mingling with the bright flavours of parsley and mint. Each bite bursts with a delightful surprise – a whisper of tang from dried limes, a unique ingredient that adds a depth of complexity unseen elsewhere. Really good.

1. Sauté Onions and Meat:
In a pot, heat vegetable oil over medium heat. Add chopped onions and sauté until golden brown.
2. Add the cubed meat and brown on all sides.
3. Add Herbs and Spices:
4. Stir in the chopped celery, fresh parsley, fresh mint, and crushed dried fenugreek leaves.
5. Add ground turmeric, salt, and pepper. Mix well to combine.
6. Dilute with Water:
Mix the tomato paste in water and pour it into the pot. Add more water if needed to cover the ingredients.
7. Simmer:
Cover the pot and let the stew simmer over low to medium heat for 1.5 to 2 hours, or until the meat is tender.
8. Finish with Lemon Juice:
Stir in lemon juice just before serving to add a fresh, citrusy flavour.
9. Serve:
Khoresht-e Karafs is traditionally served over steamed rice.

FALOODEH SHIRAZI

SERVES
2

METHOD
PAN

TIME
2 hour 30mins

DIFFICULTY
2/10

Journey to Shiraz and discover Faloodeh, a refreshing escape from summer's heat. Unlike ordinary desserts, this has noodles! Imagine translucent rice noodles in a bed of icy, rose-scented syrup. A dollop of creamy lime sherbet or tart lime juice adds a great contrast, balancing the rose's perfume.
Faloodeh offers a twist on shaved ice desserts. A Persian staple, this light dessert is perfect for a hot day or a spicy meal's sweet ending.

1. Cook the rice noodles or vermicelli according to the package instructions. Drain and let them cool.
2. In a saucepan, combine water and sugar. Bring to a boil, stirring until the sugar dissolves completely.
3. Remove from heat and let the sugar syrup cool.
4. In a large bowl, mix the cooked and cooled rice noodles with rose water and lime juice.
5. Pour the sugar syrup over the noodle mixture and stir well to combine.
6. Place the mixture in the refrigerator and let it chill for at least 2-3 hours.
7. Serve Faloodeh Shirazi in bowls, garnished with chopped pistachios or almond slivers.

INGREDIENTS:

1 cup rice noodles or vermicelli

2 cups water

1 cup sugar

1/2 cup rose water

Juice of 2-3 fresh limes

Chopped pistachios or almond slivers for garnish

Sour cherry syrup or cherry juice (optional)

Ancient Minoan

Welcome to the world of ancient Minoan cuisine! The Minoans, who lived on the island of Crete from around 2600 to 1100 BCE, had a diet that was both simple and sophisticated, featuring a wide variety of fresh vegetables, fruits, grains, and seafood.

One of the most important ingredients in Minoan cuisine was olive oil. The Minoans were known for their olive groves, and they used olive oil to cook with, as well as for medicinal and cosmetic purposes.

Another staple in the Minoan diet was bread, which was often made with barley or wheat flour. Bread was served with a variety of toppings, such as honey, cheese, and fresh herbs.

Minoan cuisine also featured a wide variety of vegetables, including tomatoes, eggplants, peppers, and onions. These vegetables were often served in simple

dishes, such as roasted vegetables or grilled skewers.

Seafood was also a key part of the Minoan diet, with fish and shellfish being caught and consumed regularly. Octopus was a particularly popular ingredient and was often served grilled or boiled.

Cheese was another important part of Minoan cuisine, with feta and ricotta being the most common types. Cheese was often used as a topping for bread, or as an ingredient in savoury pies and casseroles.

If you're looking to recreate some classic Minoan dishes in your kitchen, try making a simple tomato and cucumber salad with a drizzle of olive oil and lemon juice, or grill some octopus with fresh herbs and lemon for a flavourful seafood dish.

While Minoan cuisine may not be as well-known as some other ancient cuisines, its focus on fresh, simple ingredients and its use of olive oil and cheese make it a delicious and healthy option for modern-day cooks. So come and explore the flavours of ancient Crete, and discover how the Minoans created a cuisine that was both delicious and sustainable.

DID YOU KNOW...

Fashionable Frescoes: Minoan frescoes are known for their vibrant colours and detailed depictions of daily life. Interestingly, these frescoes showcase a remarkable variety of clothing styles, suggesting Minoans placed a high value on fashion and personal appearance. Both men and women wore elaborate jewellery and adorned themselves with intricate hairstyles.

SERVES
2

METHOD
PAN

TIME
15 mins

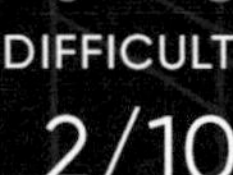

DIFFICULTY
2/10

INGREDIENTS:

4 eggs
1/4 cup of milk
1/4 cup of feta cheese, crumbled
2 tbsp of fresh herbs, such as dill, parsley, or mint
Salt and pepper, to taste
4 slices of whole-grain bread
Olive oil, for cooking

Honey, for drizzling
Crushed dried rose petals for garnish (optional)

Ancient Crete craved fresh flavours: olive oil, honey, grains, and herbs. Cretan Eggs, or Strapatsada, takes a classic breakfast and adds unexpected twists. Imagine fluffy scrambled eggs bursting with juicy tomatoes, creamy feta crumbles, and vibrant green onions. Each bite surprises - soft eggs meet tangy feta, with pops of sweetness from tomatoes. But here's the kicker: honey! It's a delicious hallmark. A sprinkle of oregano adds depth, making you wonder why you haven't tried this before.

Cretan Eggs are unique. Fresh, seasonal ingredients are key. Juicy tomatoes add acidity and sweetness, unlike plain scrambled eggs. Generous feta brings creamy richness and salty tang, perfectly complementing the other flavours. This dish celebrates fresh ingredients, simple cooking, and the humble egg's endless possibilities. One bite, and you'll be saying "Yia sas!" and dreaming of the Mediterranean.

1. Start by whisking together the eggs, milk, crumbled feta cheese, fresh herbs, salt, and pepper in a mixing bowl.
2. Heat a non-stick skillet over medium heat and add a drizzle of olive oil.
3. Pour the egg mixture into the skillet and cook, stirring occasionally, until the eggs are set and lightly golden.
4. Toast the slices of whole-grain bread.
5. Serve the scrambled eggs on top of the toasted bread, drizzled with honey.

QUOTE...

"The Minoans were a peaceful and prosperous civilisation, fostering trade and cultural exchange throughout the Mediterranean. Their legacy reminds us of the potential for cooperation and progress in the ancient world."

- Peter Green

Fakes (pronounced fah-KÉS) is one of the oldest recipes from the Minoan culture. Essentially, it's the original Lentil Soup and was a common meal among all levels of society. Simple and nutritious, it's both hearty and heartwarming. Cretan Fakes is a delicious blend of textures and flavours. Adjust the vegetables to your liking, add a pinch of dried herbs for extra depth, or even serve it with a dollop of creamy yogurt for a touch of coolness.

1. In a large pot, heat olive oil over medium heat. Add the chopped onion and cook until softened about 3 minutes. Stir in the minced garlic and cook for another minute, until fragrant.
2. Add the grated tomato, diced potato (if using), and rinsed lentils to the pot. Pour in the vegetable broth, bay leaf, and dried oregano. Season with salt and pepper to taste.
3. Simmer and Thicken: Bring the soup to a boil, then reduce heat to low and simmer for 30-40 minutes, or until the lentils are tender and the soup has thickened.
4. Remove the bay leaf and adjust seasonings with additional salt, pepper, or a squeeze of fresh lemon juice (optional). Garnish with chopped fresh parsley or dill for extra flavour and colour.

INGREDIENTS:

½ cup brown lentils (rinsed)
½ cup chopped red onion
2 cloves garlic, minced
1 large tomato, grated
1 tbsp olive oil
6 cups vegetable broth
1 small potato, peeled and diced (optional)
1 bay leaf
½ teaspoon dried oregano
Salt and black pepper to taste
Fresh lemon juice, for serving (optional)
Chopped fresh parsley or dill, for garnish (optional)

WOULD YOU RATHER…

Dance with a charging bulls or handle and worship snakes?

Chtapodhi Marinato

SERVES
2

METHOD
OVEN

TIME
2 hours

DIFFICULTY
4/10

INGREDIENTS:

1 whole octopus, cleaned and gutted

2-3 tablespoons of olive oil

1 onion, chopped

3 garlic cloves, minced

1-2 tbsp of tomato paste

1-2 tbsp of red wine vinegar

1-2 tbsp of honey

1-2 tsp of dried oregano

Salt and pepper to taste

One of the most ancient seafood recipes from the Minoan culture is this delicious Marinated Octopus. A dish that was enjoyed by the ancient seafarers who lived on the island of Crete over 3,000 years ago. A harmonious balance of Mediterranean flavours with a touch of tanginess and herbal freshness.

1. Preheat the oven to 350°F.
2. In a large pot, bring water to a boil, and then reduce the heat to medium.
3. Add the whole octopus to the pot and simmer for about 30 minutes, until it is tender.
4. Remove the octopus from the pot and cut it into bite-sized pieces.
5. In a separate pan, heat the olive oil over medium heat.
6. Add the chopped onion and garlic and cook until the onion is soft.
7. Add the tomato paste, red wine vinegar, honey, and dried oregano, and stir until everything is well combined.
8. Add the cut-up octopus to the pan and toss until it is coated in the sauce.
9. Season with salt and pepper to taste.
10. Transfer the octopus and sauce to a baking dish and bake for 15-20 minutes, until the sauce has thickened and the octopus is heated through.

Anthotyro

SERVES
2

METHOD
OVEN

TIME
25 mins

DIFFICULTY
2/10

One of the most famous desserts in ancient Crete was a sweet and creamy cheese called Anthotyro. This fresh, whey-based cheese is made from sheep or goat milk, offering a delicate flavour with a slightly tangy undertone, making it a versatile and beloved component in various Greek dishes to this day. The Minoans loved it and it was often served drizzled with honey and topped with nuts and fruit..
Here's a unique and delicious way to try it.

1. Preheat your oven to 350°F (180°C).
2. Crumble the cheese into a mixing bowl and stir it with a spoon until it becomes smooth and creamy.
3. Transfer the cheese mixture to a shallow baking dish.
4. Drizzle the honey over the cheese, making sure to cover the entire surface.
5. Sprinkle the chopped walnuts over the honey.
6. Bake the dish in the oven for 10-15 minutes, or until the cheese is slightly browned and the honey is caramelised.
7. Allow the dish to cool for a few minutes before serving.
8. Garnish with fresh fruit before serving. Enjoy your sweet and creamy Cretan dessert!

INGREDIENTS:

450g (1lb) anthotyro cheese(or ricotta cheese)

1/2 cup of honey

1/2 cup of walnuts, chopped

Fresh fruit (such as figs, grapes, or pomegranate seeds) for garnish

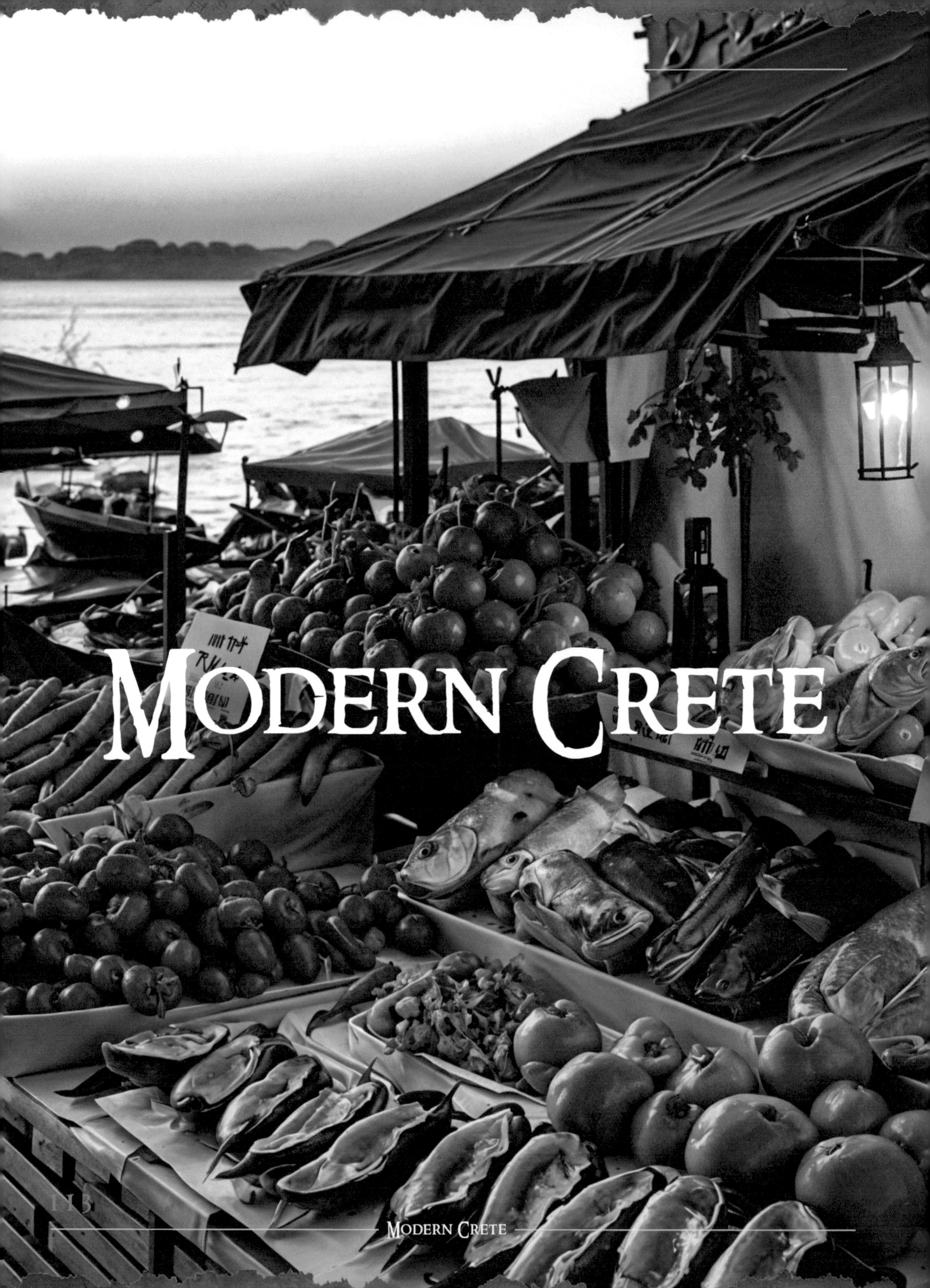

Modern Crete

In modern times, Cretan cuisine is a unique blend of traditional flavours and modern influences. Popular dishes include dakos, a salad with barley rusks, tomatoes, and feta cheese, and kalitsounia, small pies filled with herbs and cheese. The use of spices such as cinnamon, cumin, and allspice add depth and complexity to many dishes.

One of the unique aspects of Cretan cuisine is the use of local and seasonal ingredients. Fresh herbs, vegetables, and fruits are used in abundance, as well as the famous Cretan olive oil. The island's rich history of dairy farming has also led to the development of unique dairy products, such as graviera cheese and anthotyro cheese.

Despite modern influences, Cretan cuisine still holds onto its traditional roots. Many families continue to use family recipes that have been passed down for generations, and food plays an important role in Cretan culture and hospitality. Overall, Cretan cuisine is a delightful mix of ancient and modern flavours, with unique dishes and ingredients that set it apart from other cuisines.

Whether you're a seasoned cook or a beginner, there's no shortage of delicious flavours to explore in Cretan cuisine. So gather your ingredients and get ready to experience the vibrant and flavourful world of Cretan cooking!

DID YOU KNOW...

Rites of Spring... with Knives? The "Antartes" (rebels) tradition lives on in some Cretan villages. During Easter celebrations, young men dress in black clothing and brandish knives symbolically representing Cretan rebels who fought against Ottoman rule. While the practice is less widespread than in the past, it remains a powerful symbol of Cretan resistance and cultural identity.

SFAKIANOPITA

SERVES
8

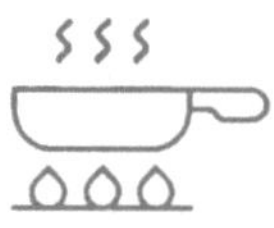

METHOD
PAN

TIME
1 hour 30 mins

DIFFICULTY
3/10

INGREDIENTS:
For the dough:
3 cups all-purpose flour
1/2 tsp salt
1/2 tsp sugar
1/2 tsp dry yeast
1/4 cup olive oil
1 cup warm water

For the filling:
2 cups crumbled feta cheese
1/2 cup chopped fresh parsley
1/2 cup chopped fresh dill
2 eggs
1/2 tsp black pepper
Olive oil, for frying

It's a Cretan cheese pie with a twist! Golden brown pastry that shatters with a satisfying crack as you cut into it. Inside, nestled in a bed of thin, almost crepe-like dough, is a creamy haven of crumbled Myzithra cheese. This isn't your average mozzarella – Myzithra boasts a tangy, ricotta-like flavour that perfectly complements the crispy exterior. A hint of cinnamon and sesame seeds adds a touch of warmth and earthy depth, making every bite an unexpected delight.

1. In a mixing bowl, combine the flour, salt, sugar, and dry yeast. Mix well.
2. Add the olive oil and warm water to the bowl. Mix until the ingredients come together into a dough.
3. Knead the dough on a lightly floured surface for about 10 minutes, until it is smooth and elastic.
4. Place the dough in a bowl and cover it with a damp cloth. Let it rest in a warm place for about 1 hour.
5. In a separate mixing bowl, mix the crumbled feta, chopped parsley, chopped dill, eggs, and black pepper.
6. Divide the dough into small balls (gold ball sized)
7. Flatten each ball to 1/4 inch thickwith a rolling pin.
8. Place a spoonful of the filling in the center of each.
9. Fold the edges of the dough up and over the filling, forming a small pouch. Pinch the edges together to seal the pouch.
10. Heat some olive oil in a frying pan over medium-high heat.
11. Fry the Sfakianopita in the hot oil, a few at a time, until they are golden brown on both sides.
12. Serve the Sfakianopita warm, with a dollop of Greek yogurt on top, if desired.

QUOTE...
"I felt once more how simple and frugal a thing is happiness: a glass of wine, a roast chestnut, a wretched little brazier, the sound of the sea. Nothing else."
-Nikos Kazantzakis

Dakos Salad

SERVES
2

METHOD
BOWL

TIME
15mins

DIFFICULTY
1/10

Greek salad has made a name for itself. Everyone knows what it is... but what about the Cretan salad? Personally, I think it's even better than its Greek counterpart and deserves more recognition. If you're looking for the taste of summer, Dakos Salad is sunshine on a plate. Fresh, salty, and savoury... it will transport you straight to the Aegean coast.

1. Soak the Cretan barley rusks (paximadia) in water for a few seconds to soften them, then drain them well.
2. Place the soaked rusks on a plate or in a shallow bowl.
3. In a mixing bowl, combine the diced tomatoes, sliced red onion, diced cucumber, and diced green bell pepper.
4. Add the chopped kalamata olives to the mixing bowl and mix well.
5. Drizzle the extra-virgin olive oil and red wine vinegar over the salad, and season with salt and freshly ground black pepper to taste.
6. Mix the salad well to combine all the ingredients.
7. Spoon the salad over the soaked Cretan barley rusks, making sure to distribute the vegetables evenly.
8. Sprinkle the crumbled feta cheese over the salad.
9. Garnish with fresh oregano leaves, if desired.

Serve the Cretan salad immediately, while the barley rusks are still slightly crunchy.

INGREDIENTS:

4 large ripe tomatoes, diced
1 small red onion, thinly sliced
1 cucumber, diced
1 green bell pepper, seeded and diced
8-10 kalamata olives, pitted and chopped
1/2 cup crumbled feta cheese
4-6 Cretan barley rusks (paximadia)
1/4 cup extra-virgin olive oil
2-3 tbsp red wine vinegar
Salt and freshly ground black pepper
Fresh oregano, for garnish (optional)

WOULD YOU RATHER...
Live on a Mediterranean Island or live on tropical Pacific Island?

APAKI

SERVES
4

METHOD
GRILL

TIME
5 hours

DIFFICULTY
4/10

INGREDIENTS:

450g (1lb) Pork tenderloin

1/4 cup olive oil

2 tbsp honey

2 tbsp red wine vinegar

2 tsp smoked paprika

2 tsp dried oregano

1 tsp garlic powder

1 tsp onion powder

1/2 tsp salt

1/4 tsp black pepper

Meat lovers, gather round for a taste of Cretan tradition! This traditional Cretan smoked pork is marinated with aromatic herbs and spices before being air-dried and smoked, resulting in a uniquely flavoured, tender, and smoky meat that embodies the essence of Cretan gastronomy. Perfect for enjoying on its own as an appetizer with a drizzle of olive oil and crusty bread, or incorporated into omelettes, salads, or pasta dishes for a smoky and savoury kick. Amazing stuff.

1. In a small bowl, whisk together the olive oil, honey, red wine vinegar, smoked paprika, oregano, garlic powder, onion powder, salt, and black pepper to make a marinade.
2. Place the pork tenderloin in a large resealable plastic bag.
3. Pour the marinade over the pork, seal the bag, and shake to coat the pork evenly.
4. Refrigerate the pork for at least 2 hours, or up to overnight.
5. Preheat a smoker or grill to 225°F (110°C).
6. Remove the pork from the marinade and discard the excess marinade.
7. Place the pork on the smoker or grill and smoke for 2-3 hours, or until the internal temperature of the pork reaches 145°F (63°C).
8. Remove the pork from the smoker or grill and let it rest for 10-15 minutes before slicing.
9. Serve the Apaki hot or at room temperature with your favourite sides.

Gamopilafo

SERVES
6

METHOD
POT

TIME
1 hour

DIFFICULTY
2/10

Travel to Crete and savour Gamopilafo, a wedding pilaf rich in history and flavour. This dish is a vibrant bowl of textures and tastes.

Fluffy, golden rice studded with vibrant fruits and nuts. Plump raisins and apricots offer a touch of sweetness. A hint of cinnamon and fragrant herbs weaves its magic throughout, creating an enticing aroma. Gamopilafo offers a unique Cretan twist on rice dishes that'll transport you to the heart of the Mediterranean.

INGREDIENTS:

1 cup short-grain rice
4 cups water
1 cup sugar
1 cup mixed nuts (such as almonds, walnuts, or pistachios), chopped
1/2 cup raisins
1/2 cup dried apricots, chopped
1/2 cup dried figs, chopped
1 tsp ground cinnamon
1/2 tsp ground cloves
Zest of one orange
Zest of one lemon
1/2 cup olive oil
Powdered sugar for dusting (optional)

1. Rinse the rice under cold water until the water runs clear.
2. In a large pot, combine the rice and water. Bring to a boil, then reduce the heat to low and simmer until the rice is cooked and the water is absorbed.
3. In a separate bowl, mix the sugar, chopped nuts, raisins, dried apricots, dried figs, ground cinnamon, ground cloves, orange zest, lemon zest, and olive oil.
4. Add the sweet mixture to the cooked rice and stir well to combine.
5. Place the pot over low heat and let it simmer, stirring occasionally until the flavours meld and the mixture thickens to a pudding-like consistency.
6. Once the Gamopilafo reaches the desired consistency, remove it from heat.

Serve the dessert warm or at room temperature.

Ancient Incan

Welcome to the ancient world of Incan cuisine! The Inca civilisation, which flourished in South America from the 13th to the 16th century, had a rich and diverse culinary tradition that incorporated a wide variety of ingredients and cooking techniques.

One of the most important crops in Incan cuisine was maize, or corn, which was used in a variety of dishes, including tamales and chicha, a fermented corn beverage. The Incas also cultivated a wide variety of potatoes, which were used in soups, stews, and roasted dishes.

Another staple in Incan cuisine was quinoa, a protein-rich grain that was used in a variety of dishes, including porridge and salads. The Incas also used a variety of beans and legumes, such as fava beans and lentils, in their cooking. Meat was a less common ingredient in Incan cuisine, as the Incas primarily relied on agriculture for their food. However, llama and alpaca meat were occasionally consumed and were often roasted or grilled over an open fire. One of the most distinctive features of Incan cuisine was its use of spices and herbs, such as aji peppers and huacatay, a type of mint. These ingredients were used to add depth and flavour to dishes and were often incorporated into sauces and marinades.

If you want to explore the flavours of ancient Incan cuisine, why not try making some classic dishes? One popular dish is ceviche, a seafood dish that is typically made with raw fish marinated in lime juice and spices. Another popular dish is lomo saltado, a stir-fry made with beef, tomatoes, onions, and spices. So come and discover the rich and diverse flavours of ancient Incan cuisine. Whether you're looking for hearty soups and stews, or flavourful salads and seafood dishes, Incan cuisine is sure to delight your taste buds and transport you to a land of history and culture.

DID YOU KNOW...

A Feast for the Dead: The Incas held elaborate ceremonies to honour their deceased ancestors. Mummies of revered leaders were periodically brought out, dressed in fine clothing, and even offered food and drink. This practice, called "capac hucha," represented a way to maintain a connection with the dead and seek their continued guidance and protection.

SERVES
2

METHOD
PAN

TIME
25 mins

DIFFICULTY
2/10

INGREDIENTS:

1 cup of quinoa, rinsed
2 cups of water
1/4 cup of honey
1/4 cup of chopped nuts, such as almonds, walnuts, or pecans
1/4 cup of dried fruit, such as raisins or cranberries
1/2 teaspoon of ground cinnamon
1/4 teaspoon of ground cardamom
1/4 teaspoon of salt
Milk, for serving

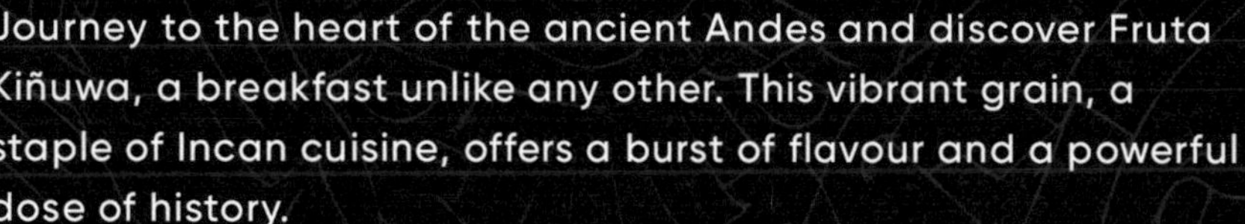

Journey to the heart of the ancient Andes and discover Fruta Kiñuwa, a breakfast unlike any other. This vibrant grain, a staple of Incan cuisine, offers a burst of flavour and a powerful dose of history.
Each bite pops with a delightful contrast: the fluffy grain giving way to a burst of juicy fruit, its sweetness balanced by a hint of earthiness. The tiny, edible seeds within add a playful crunch, creating a captivating textural dance.
The perfect harmony of sweet and tart with a distinct earthiness. This ancient treasure is a nutritional powerhouse, boasting protein, antioxidants, and Vitamin C, leaving you energized and ready to conquer the day.

1. Start by combining the quinoa, water, honey, chopped nuts, dried fruit, cinnamon, cardamom, and salt in a medium saucepan.
2. Bring the mixture to a boil over medium-high heat.
3. Reduce the heat to low, cover the saucepan with a lid, and simmer for about 15-20 minutes, or until the quinoa is tender and the liquid has been absorbed.
4. Fluff the quinoa with a fork.
5. Serve the quinoa in bowls, drizzled with a little more honey and topped with a splash of milk.

QUOTE...

"I felt sure we could gain the upper hand by putting ourselves in the mindset of the Incas."

-Tahir Shah

Looks like a layer cake, but it's not. Potato, avacado, prawns... Aji Amarillo peppers are the star of the show in Causa Rellena. Their vibrant yellow colour and smoky heat add a unique twist to the familiar potato. Plus, the customizable fillings allow you to tailor it to your taste.

Light and satisfying, Causa Rellena is perfect as a summer side or main. It's easy to make – whip up the mashed potatoes, choose your favourite filling, and assemble your colourful creation.

1. In a bowl, mix the mashed potatoes, aji amarillo paste, lime juice, salt, and pepper until well combined.
2. In another bowl, mix the cooked shrimp, diced avocado, red onion, mayonnaise, cilantro, and green onion.
3. Grease a rectangular baking dish and layer half of the potato mixture on the bottom.
4. Add the shrimp mixture on top of the potatoes and spread evenly.
5. Cover with the remaining potato mixture and smooth out the top.
6. Refrigerate for at least an hour to set.
7. Cut the Causa Rellena into rectangular pieces and serve cold with a side of lettuce and tomato salad.

INGREDIENTS:

1kg (2lb) of yellow potatoes, boiled and mashed
2 tbsp of aji amarillo paste (Peruvian yellow chilli paste)
1/4 cup lime juice
Salt and pepper to taste
450g (1lb) cooked shrimp, peeled and deveined
1 avocado, diced
1 red onion, diced
1/2 cup of mayonnaise
1/4 cup of chopped cilantro
1/4 cup of chopped green onion

WOULD YOU RATHER...
Live in an isolated community on a lake (like Titicaca) on a mountain (like Machu Pichu) or in the Jungle (in a tribal setting)?

SERVES

2

METHOD

OVEN

TIME

2 hours

DIFFICULTY

5/10

INGREDIENTS:

2 whole guinea pigs, cleaned and gutted
1/4 cup white wine vinegar
1/4 cup soy sauce
1 tbsp ground cumin
1 tbsp dried oregano
1 tbsp paprika
Salt and pepper, to taste
4 garlic cloves, minced
1/4 cup vegetable oil
2 red onions, sliced
2 bell peppers, sliced
2 tomatoes, sliced

Travel to the heart of Peru and discover Cuy al Horno, a dish steeped in history. This roasted guinea pig, a traditional source of protein in the Andes, offers a unique and flavourful adventure for the tastebuds.

Don't get freaked out! The tender meat boasts a surprisingly rich, savoury flavour unlike any other. The magic lies in the fragrant marinade.

Skip the ordinary roasts and explore the unique flavours of the Andes. Cuy al Horno, traditionally served with huacatay sauce and fluffy rice, is a complete Peruvian experience.

1. Preheat the oven to 375°F (190°C).
2. In a small bowl, whisk together the white wine vinegar, soy sauce, cumin, oregano, paprika, salt, pepper, minced garlic, and vegetable oil.
3. Rub the guinea pigs with the spice mixture, making sure to coat them evenly.
4. Stuff each guinea pig with the sliced onions, bell peppers, and tomatoes.
5. Place the guinea pigs on a baking sheet or roasting pan and cover them with foil.
6. Roast the guinea pigs in the preheated oven for 45 minutes to 1 hour, or until they are cooked through and tender.
7. Remove the foil and roast the guinea pigs for an additional 15-20 minutes, or until they are browned and crispy on the outside.
8. Serve the Cuy al Horno hot with boiled potatoes and a side salad.

Lucuma & Algarrobina

SERVES

1

METHOD

MIXER

TIME

2 hours

DIFFICULTY

1/10

It may be tough to find the ingredients in some places, but if you can... do it. The first spoonful is a revelation – a burst of creamy sweetness with a subtle floral note, the magic of lucuma, the "Gold of the Incas." And the algarrobina, a dark syrup made from tara pods, adds a rich, earthy depth that beautifully complements the lucuma's sunshine-like flavour. Light and refreshing, Lucuma & Algarrobina Pudding is the perfect way to end a meal or enjoy a delightful afternoon treat. It's easy to make Peruvian magic.

1. If using fresh lucuma, peel and remove the seeds. If using frozen lucuma pulp, thaw it.
2. In a blender, combine Lucuma pulp, Algarrobo flour, honey, water, and a pinch of salt.
3. Blend until you achieve a smooth and thick pudding-like consistency.
4. Transfer the mixture to a bowl and refrigerate for at least 2 hours to allow the flavours to meld.
5. Spoon the chilled Lucuma and Algarrobo Fruit Pudding into individual bowls.
6. Garnish with a sprinkle of ground cinnamon for an extra layer of flavour.

INGREDIENTS:

1 cup lucuma pulp (fresh or frozen)

1/2 cup algarrobo (carob) flour

2 tbsp honey or sweetener of choice

1/2 cup water

Pinch of salt

Ground cinnamon for garnish

Modern Peru

Over time, Peruvian cuisine has been influenced by various cultures, including Spanish, African, Chinese, and Japanese. These influences have led to the introduction of new ingredients and cooking techniques, as well as changes in dietary restrictions.

In modern times, Peruvian cuisine is a unique blend of traditional flavours and modern influences. Popular dishes include ceviche, a dish of marinated raw fish, and lomo saltado, a stir-fry of beef, tomatoes, and onions. The use of spices such as aji amarillo, a type of chilli pepper, and cumin add heat and flavour to many dishes.

One of the unique aspects of Peruvian cuisine is the use of a wide variety of potatoes, which come in different sizes, colours, and textures. Another staple of Peruvian cuisine is the use of corn, which is used to make dishes such as tamales and chicha, a fermented corn drink.

Despite modern influences, Peruvian cuisine still holds onto its traditional roots. Many families continue to use family recipes that have been passed down for generations, and food plays an important role in Peruvian culture and hospitality.

Overall, Peruvian cuisine is a delightful mix of ancient and modern flavours, with unique dishes and ingredients that set it apart from other cuisines. Whether you're a seasoned cook or a beginner, there's no shortage of delicious flavours to explore in Peruvian cuisine. So gather your ingredients and get ready to experience the vibrant and flavourful world of Peruvian cooking!

DID YOU KNOW...

Beyond Machu Picchu: Choquequirao's Mystery: Machu Picchu is undeniably famous, but Peru boasts another enigmatic Inca city: Choquequirao. Nicknamed "the Machu Picchu in the Clouds" for its remote location and breathtaking mountain views, Choquequirao is still being actively unearthed by archaeologists. Its purpose and connection to the Inca empire remain shrouded in some mystery.

Tamales Peruanos

SERVES
5

METHOD
STEAM

TIME
2 hours

DIFFICULTY
6/10

INGREDIENTS:

4 cups cornmeal
4 cups chicken broth
1/2 cup vegetable shortening or lard
1 tsp ground cumin
1 tsp paprika
1 tsp salt
450g (1lb) pork shoulder, diced
1 onion, chopped
2 garlic cloves, minced
2 tbsp vegetable oil
1/2 cup chicken broth
1/4 cup ají amarillo paste
1/2 tsp ground cumin
1/2 tsp paprika
1/2 tsp dried oregano
1/2 tsp salt
1/4 tsp freshly ground black pepper
1 cup frozen corn kernels
1/2 cup black olives
6 boiled eggs, sliced

Banana leaves, Kitchen twine or toothpicks

1. In a mixing bowl, combine the masa harina, chicken broth or water, vegetable shortening or lard, ground cumin, paprika, and salt. Mix to a smooth dough. Cover and set aside.
2. Heat the vegetable oil in a large skillet over medium-high heat. Add the diced pork shoulder and cook for about 5-7 minutes, or until browned on all sides.
3. Add the chopped onion and minced garlic to the skillet, and cook for another 2-3 minutes, or until the onion is translucent.
4. Pour in the chicken broth, ají amarillo paste, ground cumin, paprika, dried oregano, salt, and freshly ground black pepper. Stir well to combine.
5. Add the frozen or fresh corn kernels and sliced black olives to the skillet. Cook for another 5-7 minutes, or until the mixture is thick and most of the liquid has evaporated.
6. Remove the skillet from the heat and let the filling cool for a few minutes.
7. To assemble the tamales, spread a tablespoon of the dough mixture onto a banana leaf rectangle, leaving a border of about 1 inch all around.
8. Place a spoonful of the filling in the center of the dough, and top it with a slice of boiled egg.
9. Fold the banana leaf over the filling, then fold the ends over to seal it. Tie the tamale with kitchen twine or secure with toothpicks.
10. Repeat with the remaining dough and filling.
11. Place the tamales in a steamer basket, cover, and steam for about 45-60 minutes, or until the dough is cooked through and the filling is hot.
12. Serve the Peruvian tamales hot, garnished with extra sliced boiled eggs and chopped fresh cilantro, if desired.

QUOTE...
"I would rather own little and see the world, than own the world and see little of it."
-Alexander Sattler

CEVICHE

SERVES
4

METHOD
BOWL

TIME
2hours 30mins

DIFFICULTY
2/10

Peruvian Ceviche is a delicious national treasure. This dish is a vibrant explosion of fresh flavours and textures that will have you feeling the ocean breeze on your skin. Fresh fish marinated in zesty lime juice and mingled with vibrant ingredients like red onions, coriander, and spicy aji peppers. The burst of citrus, combined with the ocean's briny essence, creates a refreshing and lively dish that embodies the vibrant spirit of Peruvian coastal cuisine. It will always remind me of Paracas

INGREDIENTS:

450g (1lb). Fresh firm white fish (such as sea bass or tilapia)
1/2 cup freshly squeezed lime juice
1 small red onion, thinly sliced
1-2 fresh hot chilli peppers (such as habanero or jalapeño)
1/2 cup chopped fresh coriander
1/4 cup chopped fresh parsley
1/2 tsp salt
1/4 tsp freshly ground black pepper
1/2 cup diced sweet potato (cooked and chilled)
1 ear of corn, boiled and cut into rounds
Lettuce leaves, for serving

1. In a mixing bowl, combine the fish pieces with the lime juice, red onion, minced chilli peppers, chopped coriander, chopped parsley, salt, and freshly ground black pepper. Mix well to coat the fish with the lime juice and seasonings.
2. Cover the bowl with plastic wrap, and refrigerate it for at least 30 minutes, or up to 2 hours, to allow the fish to "cook" in the lime juice.
3. When ready to serve, arrange the lettuce leaves on a serving platter.
4. Spoon the ceviche onto the lettuce leaves, making sure to include some of the onions and herbs with each serving.
5. Garnish the ceviche with the diced sweet potato and boiled corn rounds.
6. Serve the Peruvian ceviche immediately, with extra lime wedges on the side, if desired.

WOULD YOU RATHER…
Eat a guinea pig or eat grasshoppers?

Lomo Saltado

SERVES
4

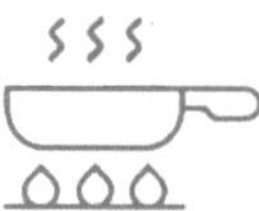

METHOD
PAN

TIME
1 hours

DIFFICULTY
4/10

INGREDIENTS:

450g (1lb) Beef sirloin or flank steak, cut into thin strips
1 red onion, sliced
1 large tomato, sliced
1 yellow chilli pepper, seeded and sliced (optional)
3 garlic cloves, minced
1/4 cup soy sauce
2 tbsp red wine vinegar
1 tbsp vegetable oil
Salt and black pepper, to taste
450g (1lb) French fries
Steamed white rice, for serving
Fresh coriander leaves, chopped, for garnish

The English have fish and chips, the Aussies have the meat pie. In Peru there is Lomo saltado. It's a popular Peruvian dish that combines marinated strips of beef, stir-fried vegetables, and French fries, all served over steamed white rice. Basic but great.
Crisp bell peppers, savoury onions, rice and aji amarillo peppers, vibrant yellow and packing a delightful punch, add a touch of smoky heat that awakens your senses. It's delicious.

1. In a large mixing bowl, combine the sliced beef, minced garlic, soy sauce, and red wine vinegar. Mix well to coat the beef evenly, and marinate for at least 30 minutes, or up to 2 hours.
2. Heat the vegetable oil in a large skillet or wok over high heat. When the oil is hot, add the marinated beef and stir-fry for 3-5 minutes, or until browned on all sides.
3. Add the sliced onion, tomato, and yellow chili pepper to the skillet. Stir-fry for another 2-3 minutes, or until the vegetables are slightly softened.
4. Season with salt and black pepper, to taste.
5. In a separate frying pan, cook the French fries according to the package instructions until crispy and golden brown.
6. To serve, place a bed of steamed white rice in a serving dish, and top with the stir-fried beef and vegetables. Garnish with the crispy French fries and chopped coriander.

TAWA TAWA

SERVES	METHOD	TIME	DIFFICULTY
12	PAN	40mins	3/10

Bite-size poppers of crispy, fried waffle with honey and strawberries. So good. You can find them all over South America. But this recipe is from the Andes Mountains of Peru. Reminiscent of empanadas with juicy chunks of seasonal fruits, like mangoes, peaches, or berries, Tawa Tawa's are good any time of day.

INGREDIENTS:

2 cups flour

2 tsp baking powder

1 tsp salt

1 tbsp butter (softened)

2 eggs (beaten)

1/2 cup water

canola oil (for frying)

honey

powdered sugar

fruit and other toppings (optional)

1. Whisk together the flour, baking powder, and salt in a large bowl.
2. Add the butter and mix well with a spatula.
3. Add the eggs and a drizzle of water. Continue mixing, and add more water as you do so. (You may need to add a bit more than half a cup.) Continue mixing until everything is incorporated.
4. Knead the dough on a floured surface until everything is smooth, about two minutes. Cover with a tea towel and allow to rest for about 10 minutes.
5. After resting, roll the dough into a thin layer (about 1/10 of an inch.).
6. Use the tip of a pairing knife to cut the dough into rhombus-shaped pieces. Cover again and allow to rest for about five minutes.
7. Heat oil in a deep fryer or in a thin layer (no more than halfway up the sides) on a frying pan.
8. Fry five or six dough pieces at a time until all of the dough has been fried. They should puff up and become golden brown. Don't forget to turn them and cook both sides.
9. Drain on a paper towel and top with honey, powdered sugar, and other toppings.
10. Serve immediately after adding toppings and enjoy!

Ancient Mayan

Welcome to the world of ancient Mayan cuisine! The Mayan civilisation, which flourished in present-day Mexico and Central America from around 2000 BCE to the 16th century, had a rich and flavourful culinary tradition that utilised a wide variety of local ingredients and cooking techniques. One of the most important ingredients in Mayan cuisine was maize, or corn, which was used in a variety of dishes, including tortillas, tamales, and stews. The Mayans also cultivated a variety of beans and legumes, such as black beans and kidney beans, which were often combined with maize to create hearty and satisfying meals.

Another staple in Mayan cuisine was chilli peppers, which were used to add heat and flavour to dishes. The Mayans also used a variety of herbs and spices, such as cilantro, cumin, and oregano, to add depth and complexity to their cooking. One of the most distinctive features of Mayan cuisine was its use of chocolate. The Mayans were the first civilisation to cultivate cacao, and they used it to make a variety of drinks and dishes, including a bitter chocolate drink called xocolatl.

If you want to explore the flavours of ancient Mayan cuisine, there are plenty of delicious dishes to try. One popular dish is cochinita pibil, a slow-roasted pork dish that is seasoned with achiote paste, orange juice, and lime juice. Another popular dish is chilmole, a spicy turkey stew that is flavoured with chilli peppers, tomatoes, and herbs.

So come and discover the rich and flavourful world of ancient Mayan cuisine. Whether you're looking for hearty stews, spicy sauces, or sweet and savoury chocolate dishes, Mayan cuisine is sure to delight your taste buds and transport you to a land of history and culture.

DID YOU KNOW...

Dental Decorations: A Status Symbol: The Mayans were obsessed with personal appearance, and their elite sported some unusual dental modifications. They might inlay jade or turquoise into their teeth, or even file their teeth into elaborate shapes. These modifications served as painful reminders of social status and religious devotion.

SERVES

2

METHOD

PAN

TIME

20 mins

DIFFICULTY

3/10

INGREDIENTS:

1 cup of masa harina (cornflour)
1/4 cup of water
1/4 cup of cooked black beans
1/4 cup of diced tomato
1/4 cup of diced avocado
1/4 cup of crumbled queso fresco or feta cheese
1 tbsp of fresh chopped coriander
Salt and pepper, to taste
Olive oil, for cooking

Journey back to the Mayan world with Masa Pancakes, a breakfast (or dessert!) unlike any other. Forget fluffy stacks – these golden gems are crafted from masa harina, a special corn flour that whispers of ancient traditions.
A soft, yet slightly crumbly texture sets these pancakes apart. A touch of honey enhances the earthy corn base.
Explore Mayan history with this simple, satisfying dish. Perfect for breakfast, brunch, or even dessert, Masa Pancakes are a window into the Mayan world.

1. Start by combining the masa harina (corn flour) and water in a mixing bowl to form a dough.
2. Divide the dough into small balls and flatten each one into a thick pancake shape.
3. Heat a non-stick skillet over medium heat and add a drizzle of olive oil.
4. Cook the masa pancakes for about 1-2 minutes on each side, or until lightly golden and cooked through.
5. Serve the pancakes topped with cooked black beans, diced tomato, diced avocado, crumbled queso fresco or feta cheese, chopped coriander, salt, and pepper.

Quote
"If I destroy you, I destroy myself. If I honour you, I honour myself."
-Hunbatz Men, Mayan

SERVES	METHOD	TIME	DIFFICULTY
4	PAN	50 mins	4/10

Explore the ancient Mayan world through Chimole, a stew unlike any other. Tender chicken or vegetables, smoky burnt chipotle peppers and a distinct sweet and chocolatey mole flavour that can only be described as.... goodness.

1. Toast the dried chilli peppers in a dry skillet over medium heat until fragrant, about 2-3 minutes per side. Remove from the heat and let cool.
2. Once the chilli peppers have cooled, remove the stems and seeds, and tear them into small pieces.
3. In a blender or food processor, combine the torn chilli peppers, tomatoes, onion, garlic, oregano, cumin, cinnamon, allspice, cloves, and 1/2 cup of the broth. Blend until smooth, adding more broth as needed to create a smooth, pourable consistency.
4. Heat the vegetable oil in a large saucepan or Dutch oven over medium-high heat. Add the chilli pepper-tomato mixture and cook, stirring frequently, for 5-7 minutes, or until the sauce has thickened slightly and darkened in colour.
5. Add the remaining 1 1/2 cups of broth and bring the mixture to a simmer. Reduce the heat to low and let simmer for 15-20 minutes, stirring occasionally, until the flavours have melded together and the stew has thickened to your liking.
6. Season the chilmole with salt, to taste.
7. Serve the chilmole hot, garnished with chopped cilantro. It can be accompanied by tortillas, rice or beans.

INGREDIENTS:

3-4 dried ancho chilli peppers
3-4 dried guajillo chilli peppers
2 medium tomatoes
1 small onion, roughly chopped
3-4 garlic cloves
1 tsp Dried oregano
1 tsp ground cumin
1/2 tsp ground cinnamon
1/2 tsp ground allspice
1/2 tsp ground cloves
1 tbsp vegetable oil
2 cups chicken or vegetable broth
Salt, to taste
Chopped fresh cilantro, for garnish

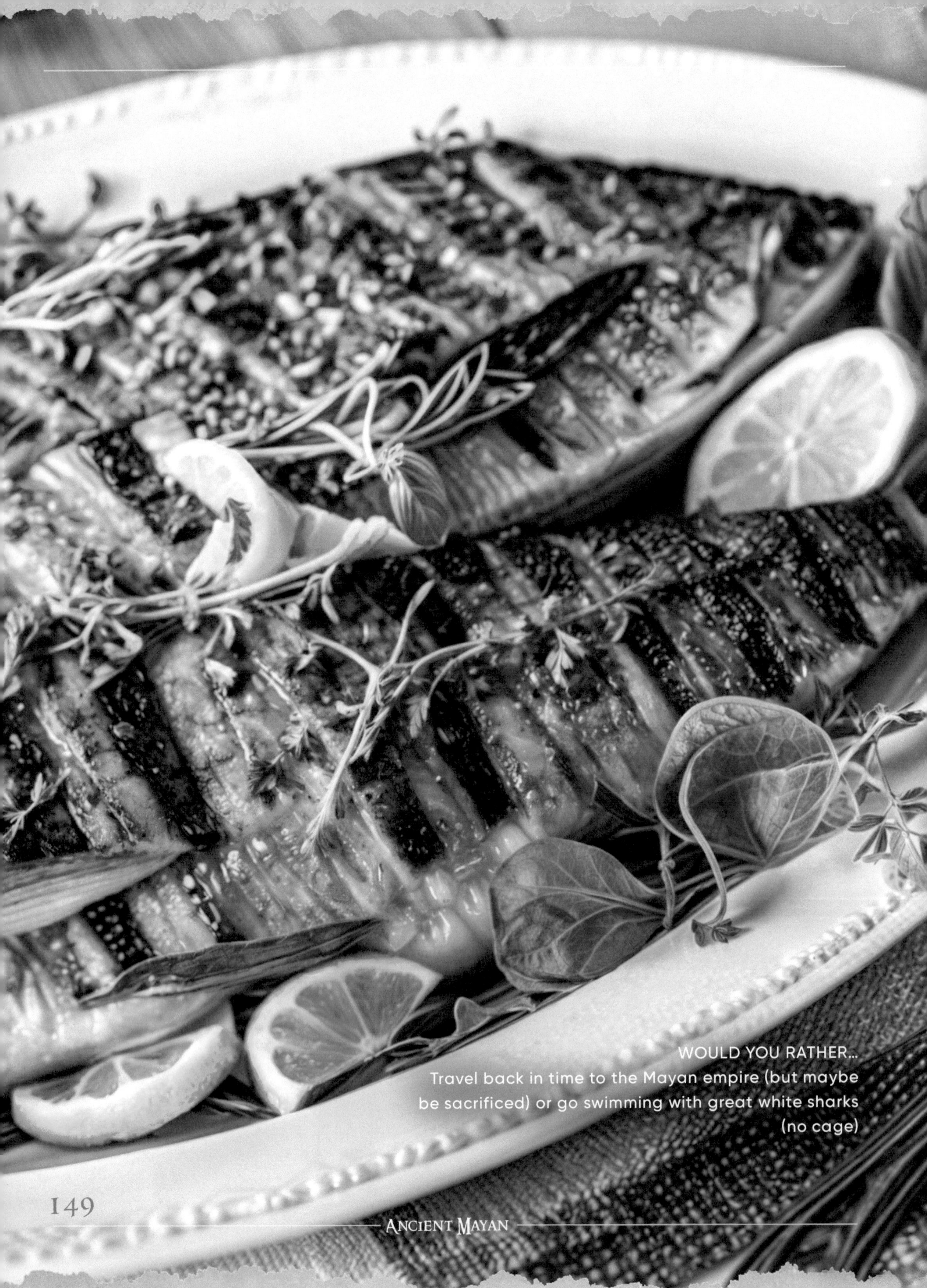

WOULD YOU RATHER...

Travel back in time to the Mayan empire (but maybe be sacrificed) or go swimming with great white sharks (no cage)

SERVES
4

METHOD
GRILL

TIME
35 mins

DIFFICULTY
5/10

INGREDIENTS:

4-6 fresh fish fillets(such as red snapper or tilapia)
2 tbsp achiote paste
1/4 cup orange juice
1/4 cup lime juice
1/4 cup white vinegar
2 garlic cloves, minced
1 tsp dried oregano
1 tsp ground cumin
Salt and pepper to taste
1/4 cup olive oil

Achiote Sauce:
1/4 cup achiote paste
1/4 cup orange juice
1/4 cup lime juice
1/4 cup white vinegar
2 garlic cloves, minced
1 tsp dried oregano
1 tsp ground cumin
Salt and pepper to taste
1/4 cup olive oil

One bite of this vibrant creation, and you'll be transported to the Yucatan Peninsula. The flavours tell a story – a story of fresh seafood, aromatic spices, and the rich cultural heritage of the Mayan people. It's a testament to their love of food and a delicious reminder of humanity's timeless connection to cuisine.

1. In a bowl, mix together the achiote paste, orange juice, lime juice,
white vinegar, garlic, oregano, cumin, salt, and pepper.
2. Add the olive oil and whisk to combine.
3. Place the fish fillets in a large dish and pour the marinade over them.
Make sure the fish is well coated.
4. Cover the dish and refrigerate for at least 2 hours (or overnight for
best results).
5. Preheat a grill to medium-high heat.
6. Remove the fish from the marinade and place on the grill. Cook for
about 5-7 minutes on each side, or until the fish is cooked through and flakes easily with a fork.
7. Serve the fish hot, topped with a generous spoonful of achiote sauce.

Sauce

1. In a bowl, whisk together the achiote paste, orange juice, lime juice, white vinegar, garlic, oregano, cumin, salt, and pepper.
2. Slowly whisk in the olive oil until the sauce is smooth and emulsified.
3. Serve the sauce alongside the grilled fish.

SERVES 4

METHOD BOWL

TIME 45 mins

DIFFICULTY 1/10

Yep! Just fruit salad. But have you seen the kinds of fruits native to the region? Holy crap, best fruit salad ever. And they knew it too. The Mayans enjoyed a variety of fruits, including pineapples, papayas, and guavas.

Prepare to be transported to a tropical paradise! This vibrant mix of tropical fruits is bursting with sweetness, tang, and a touch of Mayan magic.

Plump cubes of ruby red guava, their sweet and slightly floral flavour mingling with the juicy sunshine of papaya and pineapple. And then... A drizzle of honey adds a touch of golden sweetness, while a sprinkle of cinnamon brings a warm, fragrant depth that ties everything together beautifully.

INGREDIENTS:

1 large pineapple

2 papayas

4 guavas

Juice of 2 limes

1 tbsp honey

1 tsp ground cinnamon

1 tsp ground nutmeg

1/2 tsp ground allspice

1. Cut the pineapple in half and remove the fruit with a sharp knife or pineapple corer.
2. Peel the papayas and remove the seeds. Cut the flesh into bite-sized pieces.
3. Wash the guavas and cut them into thin slices.
4. In a small bowl, whisk together the lime juice, honey, cinnamon, nutmeg, and allspice to make a dressing.
5. Arrange the fruit on a platter or individual plates and drizzle with the dressing.
6. Chill in the refrigerator for at least 30 minutes before serving.

Modern Central America

In modern times, Central American cuisine is a unique blend of traditional flavours and modern influences. Popular dishes include pupusas from El Salvador, which are thick tortillas filled with cheese, meat, or beans, and gallo pinto from Costa Rica, a dish of rice and beans seasoned with cilantro, onion, and red pepper.

One of the unique aspects of Central American cuisine is the use of corn in many dishes. Corn is used to make tortillas, tamales, and other dishes, and is often ground into masa to make the dough used for tortillas. Another staple of Central American cuisine is the use of fresh fruits and vegetables. Papayas, pineapples, avocados, and plantains are just a few of the fruits commonly used in Central American dishes. The use of fresh herbs such as cilantro and oregano also add a unique flavour to many dishes.

Despite modern influences, Central American cuisine still holds on to its traditional roots. Many families continue to use family recipes that have been passed down for generations, and food plays an important role in Central American culture and hospitality.

Overall, Central American cuisine is a delightful mix of ancient and modern flavours, with unique dishes and ingredients that set it apart from other cuisines. Whether you're a seasoned cook or a beginner, there's no shortage of delicious flavours to explore in Central American cuisine. So gather your ingredients and get ready to experience the vibrant and flavourful world of Central American cooking!

DID YOU KNOW...

Day of the Dead Goes Digital: Central America celebrates the Day of the Dead (Día de los Muertos) with vibrant traditions, but there's a modern twist. Families increasingly create online memorials on social media to remember their deceased loved ones. These digital altars often include photos, videos, and favourite music, reflecting the evolving ways people commemorate their ancestors in the digital age.

GALLO PINTO

SERVES
4

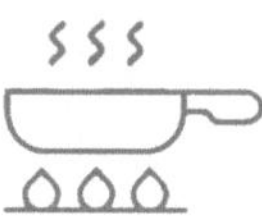

METHOD
PAN

TIME
25 mins

DIFFICULTY
2/10

INGREDIENTS:

1 cup cooked black beans (or canned black beans, drained and rinsed)
3 cups cooked white rice
1/2 red onion, chopped
2 garlic cloves, minced
1 red bell pepper, chopped
1 tbsp vegetable oil
1 tbsp Worcestershire sauce
1 tsp ground cumin
Salt and black pepper, to taste
2 tbsp chopped cilantro (optional)

Alright, amigos, gather around the table and get ready for a taste of Costa Rican goodness on a plate! Gallo pinto is a popular and traditional dish in many Latin American countries. It is a rice and beans dish that is often served for breakfast but can be enjoyed any time of day. Savoury, aromatic and earthy, it's a comforting staple and a favourite with good reason.

1. In a large skillet or wok, heat the vegetable oil over medium-high heat. Add the chopped onion, minced garlic, and chopped red bell pepper, and sauté for 2-3 minutes, or until softened.
2. Add the cooked black beans to the skillet, and stir to combine with the vegetables.
3. Add the Worcestershire sauce and ground cumin to the skillet, and stir to distribute the flavours.
4. Add the cooked white rice to the skillet, and stir to combine with the beans and vegetables. Season with salt and black pepper, to taste.
5. Cook the rice and bean mixture for 5-10 minutes, stirring occasionally, until the flavours are well combined and the rice is slightly crispy.
6. Serve the gallo pinto hot, garnished with chopped cilantro (if desired). Enjoy this delicious and satisfying dish as a main course or as a side dish with eggs, avocado, or plantains.

QUOTE...
"Central America is a land of opportunity, with a young population brimming with talent and a growing focus on innovation and entrepreneurship."
- Luis Alberto Moreno

CHANCHO CON YUCCA

SERVES
4

METHOD
POT

TIME
30 mins

DIFFICULTY
2/10

A delicious street food from Nicaragua is Chancho con Yucca. It consists of pork stewed in a flavourful spicy sauce, served with the buttery texture of cooked yucca root. If I ever mention I'm making this, friends and family just start showing up at the door. It's that good.
Originally from the Yucatan Peninsula, this is a dish that's both comforting and exciting. Forget your average pulled pork or boiled cassava – this is a punch of slow-cooked flavours where succulent pork mingles with melt-in-your-mouth yucca, all bathed in a vibrant achiote marinade.

INGREDIENTS:

1kg (2lb) pork shoulder, cut into cubes
1 red onion, chopped
4 garlic cloves, minced
2 tbsp vegetable oil
1 tbsp ground cumin
1 tbsp paprika
1 tsp dried oregano
2 cups chicken broth
Salt and black pepper, to taste
450g (1lb) yucca root, peeled and cut into chunks
Lime wedges, for serving
Sour cream

1. In a large pot or Dutch oven, heat the vegetable oil over medium-high heat. Add the chopped onion and minced garlic, and sauté for 2-3 minutes, or until softened.
2. Add the cubed pork to the pot, and stir to coat with the onion and garlic mixture.
3. Season the pork with cumin, paprika, oregano, salt, and black pepper. Stir to distribute the spices evenly.
4. Pour in the chicken broth, and bring to a boil. Reduce the heat to low, and let simmer for 1-2 hours, or until the pork is tender and the sauce has thickened.
5. Meanwhile, in a separate pot, boil the yucca root chunks in salted water for 20-25 minutes, or until soft and tender.
6. To serve, arrange the cooked yucca root on a serving platter, and top with the stewed pork and sauce. Garnish with lime wedges.

WOULD YOU RATHER...
Swim with giant Turtles or toboggan down an active volcano?

Guiso de Pescado

SERVES
4

METHOD
POT

TIME
45 mins

DIFFICULTY
3/10

INGREDIENTS:

700g (1 1/2lb) firm white fish, cut into 2-inch pieces (such as cod, halibut, or snapper)
1 large onion, chopped
2 garlic cloves, minced
2 tbsp of olive oil
1/2 tsp ground cumin
1/2 tsp ground allspice
1/2 tsp dried thyme
1/4 tsp smoked paprika
1/4 tsp of cayenne pepper
2 cups chicken or fish stock
1 can of diced tomatoes
1 can of coconut milk
1 red bell pepper, sliced
1 green bell pepper, sliced
1/4 cup of chopped fresh cilantro
Salt and pepper to taste

Seafood lovers, get your aprons on. Tonight we're setting sail on a culinary adventure with Guiso de Pescado – a fish stew unlike any you've had before.
On the Caribbean coast or in the Bay Islands, seafood and anything made of coconut dominate Honduran cuisine. No travel taste test of Honduran food is complete without fresh fish, shrimp, lobster, or the endlessly versatile conch (caracol in Spanish). But they also have some other dishes with a strong Mayan influence worth trying. This is one of the best.

1. In a large pot or Dutch oven, heat the olive oil over medium-high heat. Add the chopped onion and minced garlic and cook until the onion is translucent, about 5 minutes.
2. Add the ground cumin, ground allspice, dried thyme, smoked paprika, and cayenne pepper to the pot. Stir to combine and cook for another 1-2 minutes.
3. Add the chicken or fish stock, diced tomatoes (with their juice), and coconut milk to the pot. Bring the mixture to a simmer and cook for 5 minutes.
4. Add the sliced bell peppers to the pot and continue to simmer for another 5 minutes.
5. Season the fish pieces with salt and pepper, then add them to the pot. Gently stir the fish into the stew and cook for another 5-7 minutes, or until the fish is cooked through and flakes easily with a fork.
6. Taste the stew and adjust the seasoning as needed. Stir in the chopped cilantro.
7. Serve the stew hot, garnished with additional cilantro if desired. Enjoy!

RELLENITOS DE PLATANO

SERVES
5

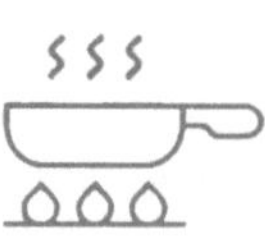

METHOD
PAN

TIME
40 mins

DIFFICULTY
3/10

Golden-brown, bite-sized pillows of fried dough waiting to be devoured. But inside hides the treasure – a decadent filling of mashed plantains, their natural sweetness coupled with the spice of cinnamon. Here's the cool bit, though! A touch of black beans, sometimes mashed or even refried, adds a subtle earthiness that perfectly complements the sweetness.

INGREDIENTS:

4 ripe plantains

1 cup black beans, cooked and mashed

1/2 cup sugar (adjust to taste)

1 tsp ground cinnamon

Pinch of salt

Vegetable oil for frying

Sugar for coating

Optional: Sesame seeds for garnish

1. Peel and boil the ripe plantains until soft.
2. Mash the boiled plantains and mix in sugar, ground cinnamon, and a pinch of salt.
3. Cook and mash black beans, sweetening them slightly with sugar.
4. Take a portion of the mashed plantains, flatten it, and spoon a bit of the sweetened black beans into the centre. Encase the beans with the plantain, forming a ball.
5. Heat vegetable oil in a pan over medium heat. Fry the filled plantain balls until golden brown.
6. Roll the fried Rellenitos in sugar while they are still warm.
7. Optionally, garnish with sesame seeds for added texture.
8. Enjoy!

ANCIENT AZTEC

Welcome to the world of ancient Aztec cuisine! The Aztecs were a highly advanced civilisation that inhabited what is now Mexico from the 14th to the 16th century. They were known for their highly organised society, advanced agriculture, and impressive culinary traditions.
At the heart of Aztec cuisine was the humble corn plant, which was transformed into a multitude of delicious dishes. One of the most popular Aztec foods was tamales, which were made by grinding corn into a dough and then wrapping it around various fillings, such as meats, beans, or vegetables. Tamales were a staple food of the Aztecs and are still a popular dish in Mexico today.

Another famous Aztec dish was pozole, a stew made from hominy (dried corn kernels), meat, and chilli peppers. Pozole was often served at religious ceremonies and was believed to have magical properties.
The Aztecs were also famous for their use of chocolate, which they consumed as a bitter beverage flavoured with spices and chilli peppers. They believed that chocolate had medicinal properties and was a powerful aphrodisiac.

In addition to corn and chocolate, the Aztecs also enjoyed a variety of other foods, including beans, squash, tomatoes, and avocados. They were also skilled at fishing and hunting and enjoyed a wide variety of seafood and game meats.

One of the most interesting aspects of Aztec cuisine is the use of insects as a source of protein. The Aztecs regularly consumed insects such as grasshoppers, ants, and maguey worms, which were considered a delicacy.
Overall, the cuisine of the ancient Aztecs was rich in flavour and history and continues to influence the cuisine of Mexico and other parts of the world today. Whether you're savouring the complex flavours of a traditional tamale, enjoying the rich spiciness of a pozole stew, or even trying out the unique taste of an insect dish, you're sure to experience the rich cultural heritage of ancient Aztec cuisine.

Did you know...
Educated Ears: Aztec education wasn't just memorization. Schools like the "calmecac" incorporated music and song as teaching tools. Students learned about history, religion, and even astronomy through musical compositions and chants. Confessions could even be delivered through song, with the melody and rhythm conveying the emotional state of the confession.

SERVES
4

METHOD
PAN

TIME
40 mins

DIFFICULTY
4/10

INGREDIENTS:

For the Dough:
2 cups masa harina (corn flour)
1 1/2 cups warm water
1/2 tsp salt

For the Filling:
1/2 cup Refried beans
1/4 cup Queso fresco (fresh cheese)
Optional: Cooked and seasoned grasshoppers (honestly just use chicken)
Toppings:
1/2 cup Salsa verde, 1/2 cup chopped onions, 1/2 cup coriander, lime wedges

Traditional Tlacoyos are crispy griddled Masa Harina tortillas stuffed with refried beans, mashed smooth and bursting with earthy goodness is just the beginning. A dollop of salsa verde, with its bright tomatillo and green chile flavours, adds a tangy counterpoint. So good.

Prepare the Dough:
1. In a bowl, mix masa harina, warm water, and salt until a soft and pliable dough forms.
2. Shape Tlacoyos: Take a portion of the dough and form an oval shape, creating a slight indentation in the center for the filling.
3. Add Fillings: Spread a layer of refried beans on one side of the oval, add crumbled queso fresco, and, if adventurous, incorporate cooked and seasoned grasshoppers or other protein.
4. Fold and Seal: Fold the masa over the filling, sealing the edges to form a stuffed oval shape.
5. Cook: Place the tlacoyos on a hot comal or griddle and cook until they develop a golden-brown crust on both sides.
6. Serve: Garnish with salsa, chopped onions, coriander, and lime wedges.

Tlacoyos offer a glimpse into the Aztec culinary palette, showcasing the use of masa with unconventional fillings. This unique breakfast reflects the cultural diversity and resourcefulness of the Aztec people.

Quote...
"Today we are at last beginning to understand the intricacies of this amazing culture, which was the equal of any in Europe in moral refinement, artistic sensibility, social complexity, and political organization."
- J. H. Elliott

Tinga de Pollo Tacos

SERVES
4

METHOD
PAN

TIME
45 mins

DIFFICULTY
3/10

A great number of the traditional dishes eaten in Mesoamerica are still popular today. Tacos, burritos, enchiladas... This basic chicken Taco recipe has been around forever.

Bursting with smoky chipotle chiles, juicy shredded chicken, and a tangy tomato sauce, these things will have you reaching for seconds (and thirds!).

The secret weapon here is the chipotle chiles in adobo sauce. These smoky peppers add a depth of flavour that's both complex and addictive, with a hint of heat that keeps things exciting.

Tinga de Pollo Tacos are a must-try for anyone who loves a flavorful, satisfying, and endlessly customizable meal.

It's a classic for a reason.

1. In a pan, sauté sliced onions and minced garlic until softened.
2. Add diced tomatoes, chopped chipotle peppers, dried oregano, salt, and pepper to the pan.
3. Simmer until the tomatoes break down and the sauce thickens.
3. Shred the cooked chicken and add it to the pan, ensuring it's well-coated with the tinga sauce.
4. Simmer for an additional 10-15 minutes.
5. Warm corn tortillas on a comal or in a dry pan.
6. Spoon the tinga de pollo onto each tortilla and top with chopped coriander and diced onions.
7. Serve Tinga de Pollo Tacos with lime wedges on the side.

INGREDIENTS:

2 cups shredded cooked chicken
1 onion, thinly sliced
2 garlic cloves, minced
1 can diced tomatoes
2-3 chipotle peppers in adobo sauce, chopped
1 tsp dried oregano
Salt and pepper to taste
Corn tortillas

Toppings:

Chopped coriander
Diced onions
Lime wedge

Would you rather...
Witness the Rise of the Aztec Empire or the Fall of the Roman Empire?

SERVES
4

METHOD
PAN

TIME
80 mins

DIFFICULTY
4/10

INGREDIENTS:

For the Pipian Rojo Sauce:
3 dried guajillo chillies, stemmed and seeded
2 dried ancho chillies, stemmed and seeded
1/4 cup sesame seeds
1/4 cup pumpkin seeds (pepitas)
3 cloves garlic
1/2 small white onion, chopped
1/2 tsp ground cumin
1/2 tsp dried oregano
2 cups chicken broth
Salt and pepper to taste
Corriander

For the Chicken:
4 bone-in, skin-on chicken thighs
Salt and pepper to taste
2 tbsp vegetable oil

Tender, juicy chicken pieces nestled in a deep red sauce so fragrant it'll fill the room with its aroma. But this isn't your average tomato sauce.
Pipian Rojo offers a rich and complex flavour profile with the earthy warmth of toasted seeds, the smoky depth of dried chillies, and a hint of garlic and cumin, creating a savoury and aromatic sauce that elevates the succulent chicken to new heights.
This Pipian Rojo recipe captures the essence of Mesoamerican flavours, incorporating indigenous ingredients like chillies and seeds. While not an exact replication of an Aztec recipe, it draws inspiration from the culinary traditions of the region.

1. Toast the guajillo and ancho chilies in a dry pan until fragrant.
2. Soak them in hot water for about 15-20 minutes.
3. In a blender, combine soaked chilies, sesame seeds, pumpkin seeds, garlic, chopped onion, cumin, oregano, and chicken broth. Blend until smooth.
4. Strain the sauce for a smoother consistency.
5.Season chicken thighs with salt and pepper.
6. In a large skillet, heat vegetable oil over medium-high heat. Brown the chicken thighs on both sides.
7. Pour the Pipian Rojo sauce over the browned chicken thighs. Simmer for 25-30 minutes or until the chicken is fully cooked and the sauce has thickened.
8. Serve the Pipian Rojo chicken over rice, garnished with sesame seeds and chopped coriander.

Xocoatl

SERVES
2

METHOD
SAUCEPAN

TIME
15 mins

DIFFICULTY
2/10

A hot chocolate unlike any you've ever tried. Forget the sugary, syrupy drinks of today. This is a taste of the past, a spiced and slightly bitter chocolate beverage that will tantalize your taste buds and stir your curiosity.

Xocolatl, meaning "bitter drink" in the Nahuatl language, was a prized drink by the Aztecs and Mayans. It wasn't meant to be sweet, but rather a complex and stimulating experience. The base is ground cacao beans, brimming with a deep, earthy chocolate flavour. But here's the twist – spices like chilli pepper, cinnamon, and vanilla are whisked into the mix, creating a symphony of sweetness, heat, and warmth that awakens your senses.

1. In a saucepan over medium heat, warm the milk until it begins to simmer. Be careful not to boil.
2. Add the finely chopped (or grated) dark chocolate to the simmering milk. Stir continuously until the chocolate is completely melted and well combined with the milk.
3. Stir in honey or agave syrup (if required), ground cinnamon, ground chilli powder, nutmeg, cloves, and a pinch of salt. Adjust sweetness and spice levels to your preference.
4. Allow the mixture to simmer for about 5-7 minutes, stirring occasionally to ensure all the flavors meld together.
5. Remove the saucepan from heat and stir in the pure vanilla extract.
6. Optionally, strain the Xocoatl to achieve a smoother texture. Pour the spicy chocolate drink into cups or mugs.

INGREDIENTS:

2 cups milk (dairy or plant-based)
60g (2oz) dark chocolate, finely chopped
2 tbsp honey or agave syrup
1/2 tsp ground cinnamon
1/4 tsp ground chilli powder (adjust to taste)
Pinch of ground nutmeg
Pinch of ground cloves
Pinch of salt
1 tsp pure vanilla extract

Modern Mexico

Over time, Mexican cuisine has been influenced by a variety of cultures, including Spanish, African, and Caribbean. These influences have led to the introduction of new ingredients and cooking techniques, as well as changes in dietary restrictions.

In modern times, Mexican cuisine has evolved to include a wide range of dishes and flavours. One of the most popular modern Mexican dishes is the taco, which can be filled with a variety of meats, vegetables, and sauces. Other popular dishes include enchiladas, tamales, and mole.
Mexican cuisine is unique in its use of spices and herbs, such as cumin, oregano, and cilantro. These ingredients add depth and complexity to dishes and give Mexican cuisine its distinctive flavour profile.

Another staple of Mexican cuisine is the use of fresh ingredients, such as tomatoes, avocados, and peppers. These ingredients are often used to make salsas, guacamole, and other condiments that add flavour and texture to dishes. Despite modern influences, Mexican cuisine still holds on to its traditional roots. Many families continue to use family recipes that have been passed down for generations, and food plays an important role in Mexican culture and hospitality.

Overall, Mexican cuisine is a delicious and diverse blend of ancient and modern flavours. Whether you're a seasoned cook or a beginner, there's no shortage of delicious flavours to explore in Mexican cuisine. So gather your ingredients and get ready to experience the vibrant and flavourful world of Mexican cooking!

Did you know...

Love for Lucha Libre Goes Beyond Entertainment: Lucha Libre wrestling isn't just a spectator sport in Mexico. It's deeply embedded in popular culture. Luchadores (wrestlers) are seen as national heroes, with their colourful masks and flamboyant personalities inspiring everything from children's toys to comic books. Lucha Libre events are also a social experience, drawing families and friends together to cheer for their favourite luchadors.

HUEVOS RANCHEROS

SERVES
4

METHOD
PAN

TIME
30 mins

DIFFICULTY
3/10

INGREDIENTS:

4 corn tortillas
4 eggs
1 cup refried beans
1 cup salsa
1/2 cup shredded cheddar cheese
1/4 cup chopped fresh cilantro
Salt and pepper, to taste
120g (4oz) chorizo sausage, diced
1/2 onion, diced
1 garlic clove, minced
1 tbsp olive oil

Huevos Rancheros with chorizo! So many bold and savoury flavours. The spiciness of chorizo complementing the rich, smoky taste of the tomato-based ranchero sauce, all crowned with the creamy texture of fried eggs? Yes, please! It's a hearty and satisfying breakfast that's impossible to screw up.

1. Heat a skillet over medium heat and lightly toast the corn tortillas until they are warm and slightly crispy. Keep them warm in the oven at a low temperature while you prepare the rest of the ingredients.
2. In a separate skillet, heat the olive oil over medium-high heat. Add the diced onion and sauté until soft and translucent.
3. Add the chorizo and garlic to the skillet and cook until the chorizo is browned and cooked through, about 5 minutes.
4. In the same skillet, add the refried beans and stir to combine with the chorizo mixture. Heat the beans until they are hot and spreadable.
5. In a separate skillet, fry the eggs to your desired level of doneness.
6. To assemble, place a tortilla on a plate and spread a generous spoonful of the chorizo and refried bean mixture on top. Add a dollop of salsa and sprinkle some shredded cheese over the top.
7. Place a fried egg on top of the cheese and garnish with chopped cilantro, salt, and pepper.
8. Repeat with the remaining tortillas and ingredients.
9. Serve immediately, with optional toppings as desired.

Quote...
"There is no stranger thing in the world than a Mexican sunrise. Out there on the edge of the world, the whole sky seems to catch fire."
- D.H. Lawrence

CONCHINITA PIBIL

SERVES
6

METHOD
OVEN

TIME
8 hours

DIFFICULTY
5/10

Prepare for one of the greatest tastes of the Yucatan Peninsula! A slow-roasted pork dish so flavorful and tender, it practically melts in your mouth.
We're all familiar with tacos and burritos etc... but have you tried this?? Conchinita Pibil is very common in Mexico... not so well known to a lot of people outside Mexico... and it is delicious. A succulent, marinated, shredded pork, rich achiote paste and tangy citrus mingle with warm earthy tones, creating a taste that's unlike anything you've had before. Top it with slices of red onion and vibrant green chiles for a pop of colour, freshness, and heat, and you're there. One of my favourites.

INGREDIENTS:

1.5kg (3lb) pork shoulder, cut into 2-inch cubes
1 cup orange juice
1/2 cup lime juice
1/4 cup white vinegar
1/4 cup achiote paste
1 tbsp cumin
1 tbsp dried oregano
1 tbsp salt
1 tbsp black pepper
1/2 tsp ground cinnamon
5 garlic cloves, minced
1 large onion, sliced
2 bay leaves
2 tbsp olive oil
Banana leaves, cleaned and trimmed
1/2 cup chicken broth

1. In a large bowl, combine the orange juice, lime juice, white vinegar, achiote paste, cumin, oregano, salt, black pepper, cinnamon, garlic, onion, bay leaves, and olive oil. Mix well.
2. Add the pork to the marinade and toss to coat evenly. Cover the bowl with plastic wrap and marinate in the refrigerator for at least 4 hours, or preferably overnight.
3. Preheat the oven to 325°F.
4. Remove the pork from the marinade and discard the bay leaves. Arrange the pork in a single layer in a baking dish.
5. Pour the chicken broth over the pork.
6. Cover the pork with banana leaves, tucking the edges of the leaves under the pork.
7. Cover the baking dish with foil and bake in the preheated oven for 3-4 hours, or until the pork is tender and falling apart.
8. Remove the banana leaves and serve the pork with tortillas, pickled onions, and sliced avocado.

Would you rather...
Visit the giant crystal cave of Naica Chihuahua, or the Grutas Tolantongo (the most luxurious swimming hole in the world)?

CHILES RELLENOS

SERVES
4

METHOD
OVEN

TIME
30 mins

DIFFICULTY
2/10

INGREDIENTS:

6 poblano peppers
450g (1lb) ground beef or shredded chicken (optional)
1/2 onion, chopped
2 cloves garlic, minced
1 tsp cumin
1 tsp chilli powder
Salt and pepper, to taste
1 cup grated cheese (Oaxaca, Monterey Jack, or Cheddar)
4 eggs, separated
1/2 cup all-purpose flour
Vegetable oil, for frying
1 cup tomato sauce

1. Preheat the oven to 425°F. Line a baking sheet with parchment paper.
2. Place the poblano peppers on the baking sheet and roast them in the oven until the skin is blistered and charred, about 15-20 minutes. Turn the peppers occasionally to ensure even roasting.
3. Remove the peppers from the oven and transfer them to a large bowl. Cover the bowl with plastic wrap and let the peppers steam for 10-15 minutes.
4. Meanwhile, in a large skillet, cook the ground beef or shredded chicken over medium heat until browned. Add the onion, garlic, cumin, chilli powder, salt, and pepper, and cook until the onion is soft and translucent.
5. Remove the skins from the peppers by gently peeling them off. Make a small slit lengthwise on each pepper and carefully remove the seeds and membranes.
6. Stuff each pepper with the cooked beef or chicken mixture, and a generous amount of grated cheese.
7. In a large bowl, beat the egg whites until stiff peaks form. In a separate bowl, beat the egg yolks until light and frothy.
8. Gently fold the egg yolks into the egg whites.
9. Roll each stuffed pepper in flour to coat.
10. In a large skillet, heat the vegetable oil over medium-high heat.
11. Dip each flour-coated pepper into the egg mixture and place it in the hot oil. Fry until golden brown on all sides.
12. Drain the fried peppers on paper towels.
13. In a small saucepan, heat the tomato sauce until warm.
14. Serve the Chiles Rellenos with warm tomato sauce on top.

CALABAZA EN TACHA

SERVES
4

METHOD
POT

TIME
6 hours

DIFFICULTY
2/10

You've just finished a long hike through a bustling Mexican market, the air thick with the aroma of sizzling spices and fresh produce. Your stomach's rumbling, and you crave something sweet, comforting, and bursting with autumnal flavours. That's where Calabaza en Tacha comes in.

Calabaza en Tacha, a traditional Mexican dessert, hails from the rich culinary heritage of Dia de los Muertos celebrations. This candied pumpkin dish, simmered in a spiced syrup, offers a delightful combination of sweet, caramelized notes from brown sugar, a warm hint of cinnamon, and the tender, succulent texture of the pumpkin, creating a unique and festive treat.

INGREDIENTS:

1 small pumpkin or butternut squash, peeled, seeds removed, and cut into chunks

2 cups brown sugar

1 cinnamon stick

3 cloves

1 orange, sliced

4 cups water

1. Peel the pumpkin, remove the seeds, and cut it into chunks or wedges.
2. In a large pot, combine brown sugar, cinnamon stick, cloves, orange slices, and water.
3. Bring the mixture to a boil, stirring to dissolve the sugar.
4. Add the pumpkin chunks to the boiling syrup. Reduce heat to a simmer and let it cook for about 1 to 1.5 hours or until the pumpkin is tender and the syrup has thickened.
5. Allow the pumpkin to absorb the flavours of the syrup by letting it cool and sit in the pot for a few hours or overnight.
6. Calabaza en Tacha can be served warm or at room temperature. You can also drizzle some of the syrup over the pumpkin before serving.

Ancient Mongolian

Welcome to the world of ancient Mongolian cuisine! As a nomadic culture, the ancient Mongolians were experts in preparing hearty and flavourful dishes using the limited ingredients available to them on the vast steppes of Central Asia. Meat, dairy, and grains were staples of their diet, and their cooking techniques were designed to be practical and efficient, perfect for a culture on the move. One of the most iconic dishes of Mongolian cuisine is buuz, or steamed meat

dumplings. These delicious treats are often served at special occasions and celebrations and are a must-try for anyone interested in experiencing the unique flavours of Mongolian cuisine.
Another popular dish is khuushuur, which are deep-fried meat pies. These savoury pies are made with a crispy dough and filled with spiced minced meat, onions, and sometimes even potatoes. They are perfect for a quick snack or a filling meal on the go.

Dairy products such as yogurt and cheese also played an important role in Mongolian cuisine. A traditional breakfast might consist of hot tea and a bowl of tsuivan, a hearty noodle dish made with hand-pulled noodles, vegetables, and small pieces of meat, often topped with grated cheese. Mongolians were also skilled at cooking meat in various ways. One technique was to cook meat in a hot pot filled with broth, vegetables, and spices. This method allowed the meat to become tender and flavourful while also infusing the broth with its rich flavour. Another technique was to barbecue meat over an open flame, using a mixture of wood and dried animal dung for fuel.

Overall, Mongolian cuisine is rich in flavour, texture, and history. Whether you're enjoying a steaming hot bowl of buuz, biting into a crispy khuushuur, or savouring the complex flavours of a hot pot, you're sure to experience the unique taste of ancient Mongolian cuisine.

Quote...
"A nomad without a horse is like a bird without wings."
- Mongol proverb

UKHRIIN MAH TEM BURTGEE

SERVES
2

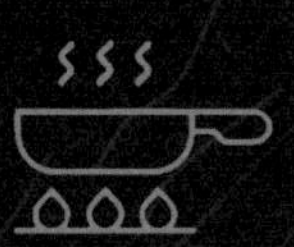

METHOD
PAN

TIME
20 mins

DIFFICULTY
3/10

INGREDIENTS:

250g (1/2lb) of thinly sliced lamb or beef
2 tbsp of butter
2 cloves of garlic, minced
1 onion, chopped
4 eggs
1/4 cup of crumbled feta cheese
Salt and pepper, to taste

Optional: chopped scallions or fresh herbs for garnish

Ancient Mongolian cuisine was heavily based on meat and dairy products, with a focus on hearty and filling dishes that could sustain nomadic lifestyles. Here's a possible recipe for a fancy breakfast that could have been enjoyed in ancient Mongolian culture:

1. Start by heating a large skillet over medium-high heat and adding the
butter to melt.
2. Add the thinly sliced meat to the skillet and cook for about 5-7
minutes, or until browned and cooked through.
3. Add the minced garlic and chopped onion to the skillet and continue cooking for another 2-3 minutes, or until the onion is softened and lightly browned.
4. Crack the eggs into the skillet and stir gently to scramble them with the meat and onion mixture.
5. Cook the eggs for about 2-3 minutes, or until they are cooked to your liking.
6. Sprinkle the crumbled feta cheese over the top of the eggs and season with salt and pepper to taste.
7. Serve the breakfast hot, garnished with chopped scallions or fresh herbs if desired.

Did you know...
Environmental Protectors: The Mongols may seem like they were all about conquest, but they actually had a strong appreciation for nature and instituted some of the world's first environmental regulations. They banned deforestation and overgrazing in certain areas and even implemented hunting restrictions to protect wildlife populations.

SERVES

2

METHOD

STEAM

TIME

45 mins

DIFFICULTY

5/10

Delicious steamed dumplings filled with meat. To this day, it is the national treasure of this vast and beautiful country. Buuz are like little pockets of comfort food happiness, bursting with flavour and a unique history. Unlike the thick, doughy wrappers of some dumplings, Buuz have a thin, almost translucent skin. The traditional way to eat them involves carefully creating a small hole in the top, allowing the steam to escape before savouring the delicious broth that collects inside. It's a little taste explosion in every mouthful!

1. In a large bowl, combine the flour, warm water, and salt. Mix well until a smooth dough forms.
2. Cover the dough with a damp cloth and let it rest for 30 minutes.
3. In a separate bowl, combine the ground beef or lamb, chopped onion, minced garlic, salt, black pepper, cilantro, and green onions. Mix well.
4. Divide the dough into 16-20 small pieces. Roll each piece into a thin circle.
5. Spoon 1-2 tablespoons of the meat mixture onto each dough circle.
6. Fold the dough over the filling and pinch the edges together to seal.
7. Arrange the buuz in a single layer in a steamer basket.
8. Steam the buuz over boiling water for 20-25 minutes, or until the dough is cooked through.
9. Serve hot with soy sauce or other dipping sauces of your choice.

INGREDIENTS:

For the dough:
2 cups all-purpose flour
1/2 cup warm water
1/2 tsp salt

For the filling:
450g (1lb) ground beef or lamb
1 onion, finely chopped
2 cloves garlic, minced
1 tsp salt
1/2 tsp black pepper
1/2 cup chopped fresh cilantro
1/4 cup chopped green onions

Would you rather...
Ride with Genghis Khan or with Alexander the Great?

Answer:
Kahn killed around 40 million. Alexander: around 300,000.

SERVES
4

METHOD
PAN

TIME
25 mins

DIFFICULTY
3/10

INGREDIENTS:

450g (1lb) ground beef or lamb

2 cups all-purpose flour

1/2 cup warm water

1/4 cup chopped onions

1 tbsp minced garlic

Salt and pepper to taste

Oil for frying

This savoury and crispy dish would have been a popular dinner option for ancient Mongolians, who often cooked their food over open fires and relied on meat for protein and energy. Khuushuur can be enjoyed on its own or with a side of vegetables or yogurt for a well-rounded meal. The fried dough offers a satisfying crunch, while the savoury filling is a delightful mix of textures – the tender ground meat mingling with the occasional pop of finely chopped onion. And the secret flavour weapon? Freshly ground black pepper. If you're an Aussie like me, it's nice to find a meat pie in the far reaches of the world.

1. In a large mixing bowl, combine the ground meat, onions, garlic, salt, and pepper. Mix well.
2. In a separate bowl, mix the flour and warm water until it forms a smooth dough. Knead for about 5 minutes.
3. Roll out the dough into a thin sheet, about 1/8 inch thick.
4. Using a round cookie cutter or a glass, cut the dough into circles about 3-4 inches in diameter.
5. Place a tablespoon of the meat mixture on one half of each circle of dough.
6. Fold the other half of the dough over the meat and seal the edges by pressing with a fork.
7. Heat oil in a frying pan over medium heat. Fry the pastries until they are golden brown, about 2-3 minutes on each side.
8. Drain on paper towels and serve hot.

SERVES
6

METHOD
PAN

TIME
40 mins

DIFFICULTY
4/10

Immerse yourself in the rich nomadic history of Mongolia with Boortsog, the country's most beloved cookie. These golden-brown pillows of fried dough have been a staple food for centuries, enjoyed by hearty nomads as they traversed the vast Mongolian steppes. A testament to the ingenuity of these communities, Boortsog offered a portable and satisfying source of energy on long journeys.

1. In a large mixing bowl, combine the flour, baking powder, salt, and sugar.
2. Add in the softened butter and mix until crumbly.
3. Slowly pour in the warm milk and mix until a dough forms.
4. Knead the dough for a few minutes, then cover and let it rest for 20 minutes.
5. Roll the dough out to about 1/4 inch thickness and cut it into small rectangles.
6. Heat oil in a large pan over medium-high heat.
7. Fry the rectangles of dough in the oil, flipping once, until they are golden brown and crispy.
8. Remove the Boortsog from the oil and place them on paper towels to drain any excess oil.
9. Brush the beaten egg on top of the Boortsog for added shine and sweetness.
10. Serve the Boortsog warm and enjoy!

INGREDIENTS:

4 cups flour

1 tsp baking powder

1/2 tsp salt

1/4 cup sugar

1/4 cup butter, softened

1/2 cup warm milk

1 egg, beaten

Oil for frying

Modern Mongolia

In modern times, Mongolian cuisine has evolved to include a variety of dishes and flavours. One of the most popular modern Mongolian dishes is khorkhog, which is a dish made with mutton cooked over hot stones. Other popular dishes include buuz, a type of steamed dumpling filled with meat and vegetables, and tsuivan, a noodle dish made with meat and vegetables.

Mongolian cuisine is unique in its use of ingredients and cooking techniques. One of the most important ingredients is meat, particularly mutton, which is used in a variety of dishes. Dairy products, such as yoghurt and cheese, are also commonly used.

Another unique aspect of Mongolian cuisine is its use of hot stones for cooking. This traditional cooking method involves heating stones over a fire, and then using them to cook meat and vegetables. The stones give the food a unique smoky flavour and help to seal in the juices. Mongolian cuisine also makes use of a variety of herbs and spices, including garlic, ginger, and cumin. These ingredients add depth and complexity to dishes and give Mongolian cuisine its distinctive flavour profile.

Despite modern influences, Mongolian cuisine still holds onto its traditional roots. Many families continue to use family recipes that have been passed down for generations, and food plays an important role in Mongolian culture and hospitality.

Overall, Mongolian cuisine is a hearty and delicious blend of ancient and modern flavours. Whether you're a seasoned cook or a beginner, there's no shortage of delicious flavours to explore in Mongolian cuisine. So gather your ingredients and get ready to experience the rich and flavourful world of Mongolian cooking!

Did you know...
Milk Mania: From Bovine to Camel: Milk is a staple food in Mongolia, consumed in various forms like yogurt (airag), fermented mare's milk (kumis), and even camel milk. These drinks are not just beverages; they're considered symbols of hospitality and are offered to guests as a sign of respect. Herding cows, sheep, camels, and horses remains a vital part of the Mongolian economy and cultural identity.

Mongolian Milk Tea

SERVES
2

METHOD
POT

TIME
20mins

DIFFICULTY
2/10

INGREDIENTS:

4 cups water

4 tbsp black tea leaves

2 cups whole milk

1/4 tsp salt (optional)

2 tsp of butter

Sugar or honey, to taste

Let's warm you up from the inside out! This morning we're looking out over the vast Mongolian steppe with a mug of something truly unique – Mongolian milk tea. Forget your fancy lattes and sugary drinks; this tea is a hearty, soul-satisfying delightful blend of both.

Sure, you've had tea with milk before, but Mongolian milk tea is a whole different story. The addition of salt and butter elevates the experience, transforming it from a simple beverage to a nourishing mini-meal.

1. In a large saucepan, bring the water to a boil.
2. Add the tea leaves to the water and let steep for 5-7 minutes.
3. Strain the tea leaves from the water and discard the leaves.
4. Return the tea-infused water to the saucepan and add the milk.
5. If desired, add the salt and butter to the tea and stir to dissolve.
6. Heat the tea and milk mixture over medium heat, stirring occasionally, until it comes to a simmer.
7. Reduce the heat to low and let the tea simmer for 5-7 minutes, stirring occasionally.
8. Remove the tea from the heat and let it cool slightly.
9. Add sugar or honey, to taste, and stir to dissolve.
10. Pour the tea into cups and serve hot.

Enjoy your delicious Mongolian Milk Tea!

Quote...
"Under the vast sky, all people are brothers."
- Mongolian proverb

GURILTAI SHUL

SERVES	METHOD	TIME	DIFFICULTY
4	POT	2 hours	3/10

INGREDIENTS:
450g (1lb) mutton or beef cut into bite-sized pieces
2 tbsp vegetable oil
2 large potatoes, peeled and diced
1 turnip, peeled and diced
2 onions, chopped
1 carrot, chopped
2 tsp ground cumin
1 tsp ground coriander
1/2 tsp dried thyme
2 tsp grated ginger
2 cloves garlic, minced
2-3 ltrs (qts)water
2-4 tbsp soy sauce
1 packet fresh or dried flat noodles
Salt and freshly ground black pepper, to taste
Chopped fresh cilantro or scallions, for garnish

1. Marinate the meat: In a bowl, combine the mutton/beef pieces with 1 tablespoon soy sauce, 1/2 teaspoon grated ginger, and 1 clove minced garlic. Marinate for at least 30 minutes (or up to overnight).
2. Heat oil in a large pot or Dutch oven over medium-high heat. Add the mutton/beef pieces and cook until browned on all sides. Remove the meat with a slotted spoon and set aside.
3. Add the onions to the pot and cook until softened, about 5 minutes. Add the carrots and cook for another 2-3 minutes.
4. Stir in the cumin, coriander, thyme, remaining grated ginger, and minced garlic. Cook for 30 seconds to release the fragrance.
5. If desired, pour in a splash of water or broth to scrape up any browned bits from the bottom of the pot.
6. Add liquids and simmer: Return the browned meat to the pot. Pour in the water and soy sauce. Bring to a boil, then reduce heat and simmer for 1-1.5 hours, or until the meat is tender.
7. Add the potatoes and turnip to the pot and simmer for an additional 15-20 minutes, or until tender.
8. According to package instructions, cook the noodles in a separate pot of boiling water. Drain and rinse with cold water if using fresh noodles.
9. Taste the soup and adjust seasonings with additional soy sauce, salt, and black pepper as needed.
10. Serve: In individual bowls, add cooked noodles, top with hot soup and meat/vegetables. Garnish with chopped fresh cilantro or scallions if desired.

Would you rather...
Spend a week with the Mongolian Shaman of Terkhiin Tsagaan Lake, or spend a week riding with the horsemen of Bogd-Khan mountain?

CHI FENG

SERVES
2

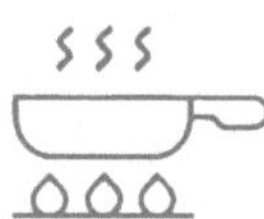

METHOD
PAN

TIME
25mins

DIFFICULTY
3/10

INGREDIENTS:

450g (1lb) lamb, thinly sliced
1/4 cup cornstarch
2 tbsp vegetable oil
1 onion, sliced
1 red bell pepper, sliced
2 green onions, chopped
3 garlic cloves, minced
1 tbsp ginger, minced
1 tbsp soy sauce
1 tbsp hoisin sauce
2 tbsp brown sugar
1 tsp red pepper flakes
1/2 cup chicken broth
Salt and pepper, to taste

Savour the sizzling delight of Mongolian Chi Feng, a vibrant dish that bursts with bold flavours. Tender slices of lamb star in this culinary adventure, mingling with a load of colourful vegetables bathed in a richly aromatic sauce. Each bite is sweet, savoury, and spicy. guaranteed to make your taste buds happy.

1. In a large bowl, toss the sliced lamb with cornstarch until evenly coated.
2. In a large skillet, heat the vegetable oil over medium-high heat.
3. Add the lamb to the skillet and cook until browned on all sides, about 3-4 minutes.
4. Remove the lamb from the skillet and set aside.
5. In the same skillet, add the onion, red bell pepper, green onions, garlic, and ginger. Cook until the vegetables are soft and fragrant, about 3-4 minutes.
6. In a small bowl, whisk together the soy sauce, hoisin sauce, brown sugar, red pepper flakes, and chicken broth.
7. Add the sauce to the skillet and stir to combine.
8. Return the lamb to the skillet and stir to coat in the sauce.
9. Cook until the sauce thickens and the lamb is cooked through, about 5-7 minutes.
10. Season with salt and pepper, to taste.
11. Serve the Mongolian Chi Feng over rice or noodles, garnished with additional green onions, if desired.

Enjoy your delicious Mongolian Chi Feng!

AARUUL

SERVES
MANY

METHOD
POT

TIME
5 days

DIFFICULTY
5/10

1. In a large pot, bring the milk to a boil over medium heat. Stir frequently with a wooden spoon to prevent it boiling over.
2. When the milk is boiling, add the kefir. Continue stirring until the milk is thoroughly curdled. You should see white clumps (curds) separated from the translucent yellow liquid (whey).
3. Remove from heat and strain out the curds. Save the whey! It's full of nutrients (you can use it in tons of ways).
4. Take a small amount of the curds and put them into a bowl. Do the same with an equal amount of curd in a second bowl. In the first bowl, stir in Sea Buckthorn jam to taste. In the second, stir in Goji berry jam (or blueberry jam) to taste. In both bowls, you want the colour to be vibrant!
5. In some moulds add a thin layer of sea buckthorn. In others petals, or goji or blueberry curd. In the remaining holes, add more unflavored curd so the amounts in each portion are level and equal. You may want to use a mould with wide patterns to make this easier. If your mould is simpler, just add in some flavoured curd first, then unflavored on top of it.
6. Put the moulds under mosquito netting (to keep bugs out) and put the moulds directly into the hottest sunlight you can find – DO NOT make this except in the Summer when the temperature is over 80 degrees, preferably even hotter!
7. Take the moulds in as the sun goes down and put them in the fridge. Repeat the cycle every day until the aaruul is rock-hard! Store anywhere, at any temperature once dry. They should last pretty much forever, as long as insects don't get to them.

INGREDIENTS:

2 ltrs (1/2 gallon) whole milk

1/2 cup authentic kefir

Sea buckthorn jam, to taste

Goji jam, to taste

Decorative moulds to pour milk curds into (optional)

Ancient Celts

Welcome to the world of ancient Celtic cuisine! The Celts, who inhabited much of Europe during the Iron Age and the Medieval period, had a rich and diverse culinary tradition that incorporated a wide variety of local ingredients and cooking techniques.

One of the most important ingredients in Celtic cuisine was grains, such as barley, wheat, and oats, which were used to make bread, porridge, and beer. The Celts also used a variety of herbs and spices, such as thyme, rosemary, and garlic, to add flavour and depth to their dishes.

Another staple in Celtic cuisine was meat, particularly beef, pork, and lamb, which were often roasted over an open fire or grilled on a spit. The Celts also hunted wild game, such as deer and wild boar, and incorporated them into their cooking.

One of the most distinctive features of Celtic cuisine was its use of dairy products, such as butter, cheese, and curds. These ingredients were used to make a variety of dishes, including cheese pies, curd tarts, and buttery breads. If you want to explore the flavours of ancient Celtic cuisine, there are plenty of delicious dishes to try. One popular dish is bangers and mash, a hearty meal made with sausages, mashed potatoes, and gravy. Another popular dish is shepherd's pie, a savoury pie made with ground lamb, vegetables, and mashed potatoes.

So come and discover the rich and diverse world of ancient Celtic cuisine. Whether you're looking for hearty stews, flavourful roasts, or sweet and savoury dairy dishes, Celtic cuisine is sure to delight your taste buds and transport you to a land of history and culture.

Did you know...

Triple Power: The Significance of the Number Three: The number three held deep symbolic meaning for the Celts. Many aspects of their society and religion were structured around triads, groups of three. This could represent the three realms of existence (earth, sky, and underworld), the three stages of life (youth, adulthood, and old age), or even the three functions of Celtic society (warriors, priests, and farmers).

SERVES

2

METHOD

PAN

TIME

15 mins

DIFFICULTY

2/10

INGREDIENTS:

4 slices of thick bread, such as sourdough or rye
2 tbsp of butter
4 slices of smoked bacon or ham
2 eggs
1/4 cup of grated cheddar cheese
Salt and pepper, to taste
Optional: sliced mushrooms, diced onions, or chopped herbs for garnish

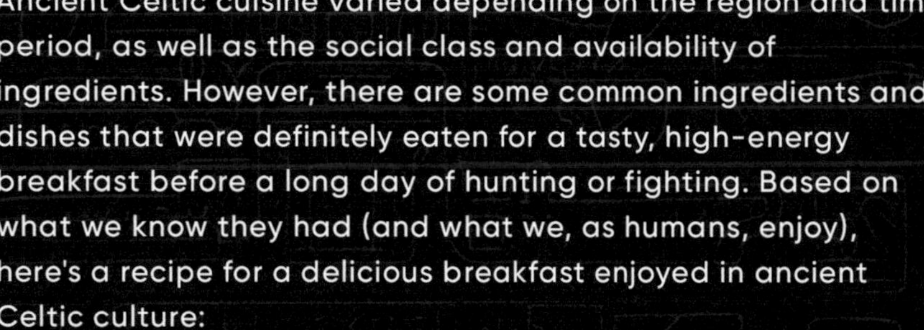

Ancient Celtic cuisine varied depending on the region and time period, as well as the social class and availability of ingredients. However, there are some common ingredients and dishes that were definitely eaten for a tasty, high-energy breakfast before a long day of hunting or fighting. Based on what we know they had (and what we, as humans, enjoy), here's a recipe for a delicious breakfast enjoyed in ancient Celtic culture:

1. Start by preheating a large skillet over medium-high heat and adding the butter to melt.
2. Add the bacon or ham slices to the skillet and cook for about 5-7 minutes, or until crispy and browned. Remove from the skillet and set aside.
3. Crack the eggs into the skillet and cook for about 2-3 minutes, or until they are cooked to your liking.
4. While the eggs are cooking, toast the slices of bread until they are lightly browned.
5. Place one slice of the toasted bread on each plate and top with a slice of the cooked bacon or ham.
6. Place one cooked egg on top of each slice of bacon or ham.
7. Sprinkle the grated cheddar cheese over the top of the eggs and season with salt and pepper to taste.
8. Optional: Garnish the breakfast with sliced mushrooms, diced onions, or chopped herbs if desired.
9. Serve the breakfast hot, with a side of fresh fruit or berries if desired.

Quote...
"Out of the silence it came, and into the silence it went back. But between the two moments there was music."
- Anonymous bard (attributed to Celtic tradition)

SERVES

4

METHOD

POT

TIME

40 mins

DIFFICULTY

2/10

Perfectly creamy, buttery mashed potatoes with earthy kale and scallions. Traditionally colcannon was served with a loin of bacon or baked ham and in our house, parsley sauce! Since we're vegetarian now I skip the ham! I usually serve this with my hearty vegetable stew or with some veggie sausages. It always goes down a treat.

1. Boil the potatoes: Place the quartered potatoes in a large pot and cover them with cold water. Bring the water to a boil over high heat, then reduce heat and simmer for 15-20 minutes, Drain the water and return the potatoes to the pot.
2. Prepare the kale: While the potatoes are boiling, wash and chop the kale (or cabbage).
3. Sauté the green onions: In a separate pan, melt 1 tablespoon of butter over medium heat. Add the chopped green onions and cook for 2-3 minutes, or until softened. Set aside.
4. Mash the potatoes: Using a potato masher or hand mixer, mash the cooked potatoes until smooth.
5. Incorporate the kale: Add the chopped kale to the pot with the mashed potatoes. You can add it raw for a slightly firmer texture, or blanch it for a few minutes in boiling water before adding it for a softer texture. Season with salt and pepper to taste.
6. Enrich the mash: Add the milk, remaining butter, and green onions (with the butter they were cooked in) to the potato and kale mixture. Stir gently to combine until well incorporated and creamy.
7. Serve: Serve the colcannon hot, topped with optional crumbled cheddar cheese. Enjoy!

INGREDIENTS:

1kg (2lb) russet potatoes, peeled and quartered
1/2 cup chopped kale (or green cabbage)
1/4 cup chopped green onions
1/4 cup milk
4 tbsp unsalted butter
Salt and freshly ground black pepper, to taste
1/4 cup crumbled cheddar cheese (optional)

Would you rather...
Bathe as often as an ancient Celt or Bathe as often as an ancient Indian?
Answer:
Both bathed very often. The Celts had a vast array of grooming tools and introduced soap to the Romans while the Ancient Indians often bathed up to three times a day.

SERVES
4

METHOD
POT

TIME
85 mins

DIFFICULTY
3/10

INGREDIENTS:

225g (1/2lb) hazelnuts, skins removed
1/2 cup salted butter
450g (1lb) boar, a nice whole piece of boar is best, but ground works fine
1 tbsp mustard seeds, lightly ground
1 to 2 cups chopped leeks
1/2 cup chopped chives
3 cups fresh greens, chopped small, kale and collard greens work well
6 cups water
3 cups wheat berries
A small bunch of sorrel
A small bunch of marjoram
1 tablespoon salt, more or less to taste

Travel back in time with this hearty and flavorful stew, inspired by the culinary traditions of the ancient Celts. Buttery hazelnuts lend a delightful crunch that complements the rich savoriness of boar meat. Leeks and chives add a touch of earthy elegance, while the subtle bite of greens provides a refreshing counterpoint. Wheat berries, a staple grain for Celts, bring a satisfying heartiness to the dish, making it a perfect meal to nourish body and soul. Imagine yourself gathered around a crackling fire, sharing stories and laughter as you savor this robust stew – a true taste of history reborn on your plate.

1. Lightly crush hazelnuts (not to a fine powder).
2. Melt half the butter in a pot (or cauldron!) over medium heat. Add hazelnuts and cook, stirring often, until fragrant.
3. Add leeks, chives, finely chopped marjoram, remaining butter, and cook 5 minutes.
4. Stir in boar (chopped into hearty chunks or ground, cook 5-10 minutes depending on size).
5. Add greens, cook 2 minutes until wilted.
6. Pour in water, simmer 20 minutes or until everything is soft.
7. Season with salt (about 1 tbsp), then add wheat berries. Cook 20-25 minutes, adding more water if needed, until berries plump and soak up most of the liquid.
8. Chop and stir through sorrel a few minutes before serving.
9. Serve with your favorite beer!

BEALTAINE CAKE

SERVES
12

METHOD
OVEN

TIME
6 hours

DIFFICULTY
6/10

Bealtaine was a festival of great significance for the Celts. Many people put out sweets for the fairies to appease them. Among those sweets was the Bealtaine cake. Warming spices like cinnamon, nutmeg, and ginger are incredible. I'm not a cake guy... but I love this.

1. Preheat oven to 350 degrees Fahrenheit.
2. Grease a large bundt pan or spring-form pan
3. Melt chocolate in a double boiler and set aside.
4. Mix milk, brandy, and vanilla.
5. Mix flour, baking powder, nutmeg, cardamom, cloves, and ginger in a separate bowl.
6. Cream the butter, then add brown sugar and beat until fluffy.
7. Add eggs, one at a time, into the butter mixture.
8. Add cooled chocolate to the butter mixture.
9. Add the flour mixture and milk mixture to the butter mixture a little at a time.
10. Pour mixture into greased bundt pan or spring-form pan.
11. Bake for approximately 50 minutes, or until done (test with a small knife), taking care not to overbake.
12. Let cake cool for 20 minutes before removing from pan, then place it into a bowl (flat side up) that is just large enough to hold it, but no larger.
13. Using a skewer, pierce the cake with 10-12 holes, being careful not to go all the way through.
14. Pour 1/3 of the amaretto over the cake. When that is absorbed, pour another 1/3 amaretto; when absorbed, pour the remainder onto the cake. This will take several hours.
15. When all of the amaretto has been absorbed, gently invert the cake onto a plate (flat side down).
16. Dust the cake with confectioner's sugar.

INGREDIENTS:

210g (7oz) all-purpose flour
2 tsp baking powder
1/2 tsp nutmeg
1/2 tsp ground cardamom
1/2 tsp ml ground cloves
2 tsp ground ginger
85g (3oz) unsweetened chocolate
1/2 cup milk
1/4 cup brandy
1/2 tsp vanilla extract
170g (6oz) butter, softened
225g (8oz) dark brown sugar
3 large eggs
3/4 cup amaretto liqueur
Icing sugar for dusting

Modern Ireland

Modern Irish cuisine has been influenced by a variety of factors, including immigration and globalisation. Today, you can find traditional Irish dishes alongside modern twists and international flavours.

One of the most iconic Irish dishes is Irish stew, made with lamb or mutton, potatoes, onions, and herbs. Other popular dishes include bacon and cabbage, boxty (a type of potato pancake), and colcannon (a dish made with mashed potatoes and cabbage or kale).

Irish cuisine is unique in its use of locally sourced, fresh ingredients. The country's mild climate and fertile soil make it ideal for growing a wide range of fruits, vegetables, and herbs. Irish dairy products, such as butter and cheese, are also highly regarded for their quality and flavour.

Another unique aspect of Irish cuisine is the emphasis on hospitality and sharing food with others. In Ireland, a warm welcome and a home-cooked meal are seen as important expressions of friendship and hospitality. Despite modern influences, Irish cuisine still holds on to its traditional roots. Many families continue to use family recipes that have been passed down for generations and traditional dishes are often served at special occasions such as holidays and family gatherings.

Overall, Irish cuisine is a delicious blend of ancient and modern flavours, with an emphasis on fresh, locally sourced ingredients and hospitality. Whether you're a seasoned cook or a beginner, there's no shortage of delicious flavours to explore in Irish cooking. So gather your ingredients and get ready to experience the rich and flavourful world of Irish cuisine!

Did you know...
Gaelic Greetings: A Revival of the Irish Language: While English is the dominant language in Ireland, there's a growing movement to revitalize Irish Gaelic (Gaeilge). Irish language classes are becoming more popular, especially among younger generations. Irish language radio stations and TV channels exist, and some areas even have Gaeltachtai (Irish-speaking regions) where Irish is the primary language of daily life.

Boxty

SERVES
2

METHOD
POT

TIME
15mins

DIFFICULTY
2/10

INGREDIENTS:

1 cup grated raw potatoes

1 cup mashed potatoes

1 cup all-purpose flour

1 tsp baking powder

1 tsp salt

1/4 cup milk

1 egg, beaten

2 tbsp butter, melted

Boxty are delectable Irish potato pancakes that capture the essence of comfort food. Imagine fluffy grated potatoes swirled with creamy mashed potatoes, all bound together with a touch of flour and enlivened by a hint of baking powder. These golden wonders are then pan-fried to crispy perfection, delivering a textural contrast that's both delightful and satisfying.

Each bite of boxty bursts with the earthy goodness of Irish potatoes. The inclusion of mashed potatoes adds a layer of richness and creaminess, creating a symphony of potato flavours that's uniquely Irish. Simple yet soul-warming, boxty are a true testament to Ireland's love for the humble spud.

1. In a large mixing bowl, combine grated raw potatoes, mashed potatoes, flour, baking powder, and salt.
2. Add in the beaten egg, melted butter, and milk. Stir everything together until the mixture is well combined.
3. Heat a large skillet over medium-high heat. Add a tablespoon of butter to the skillet and let it melt.
4. Once the butter is melted, use a ladle to pour the boxty batter onto the skillet. Cook the boxty for about 3-4 minutes on each side or until they are golden brown.
5. Repeat until you've used up all the batter.
6. Serve the boxty with your favourite toppings, such as sour cream, chives, and bacon.

Enjoy your delicious boxty!

Quote...
"The Irish are a fair people...they never speak well of themselves."
- Jonathan Swift

SPICE BAG

SERVES
2

METHOD
PAN

TIME
25mins

DIFFICULTY
3/10

IThis isn't just about satisfying your hunger; it's a delicious adventure for your taste buds. Imagine a steaming paper bag overflowing with golden-fried treasures – crispy chicken pieces mingle with fluffy fries, and slivered onions add a delightful textural contrast. But the true magic lies in the secret spice blend, a symphony of aromatic flavours ti tickle your buds.

1. Preheat your oven to 400°F (200°C).
2. Heat the vegetable oil in a deep-fryer or large pot to 375°F (190°C).
3. Fry the chips in the hot oil until crispy and golden brown. Drain on a paper towel-lined plate and sprinkle with salt.
4. In a separate pan, heat a tablespoon of vegetable oil over medium heat. Add the sliced onion and minced garlic and cook until the onion is translucent.
5. Add the chicken pieces to the pan and cook until browned.
6. In a small bowl, mix the chilli powder, smoked paprika, ground cumin, and ground coriander.
7. Sprinkle the spice mixture over the chicken and onion mixture, stirring until well-coated.
8. Transfer the chicken and onion mixture to an ovenproof dish and bake in the preheated oven for 10-15 minutes, or until the chicken is cooked through.
9. Combine the cooked chips and chicken mixture in a large bowl and toss to mix.
10. Serve your homemade Irish spice bag with your favourite dipping sauce.

Enjoy your delicious homemade Irish spice bag!

INGREDIENTS:

450g (1lb) chicken breast, cut into small pieces
450g (1lb) frozen chips (fries)
1 large onion, sliced
2 cloves garlic, minced
1 tsp chilli powder
1 tsp smoked paprika
1 tsp ground cumin
1 tsp ground coriander
Salt and black pepper to taste
Vegetable oil for frying

Would you rather...
Spend a day in the Irish countryside (when it's raining) or spend a day in an Irish Pub (when it's loud)?

CODDLE

SERVES
4

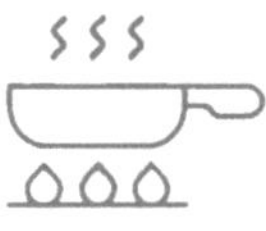

METHOD
PAN

TIME
2 hours

DIFFICULTY
2/10

INGREDIENTS:

450g (1lb) sausages

230g (8oz) bacon, diced

4 large potatoes, peeled and sliced

2 large onions, sliced

2 cups chicken stock

Salt and black pepper to taste

Fresh parsley, chopped

Irish Coddle, a hearty sausage and potato stew, has its roots in Dublin and likely emerged sometime in the 18th century. .The name coddle was originated from the slow cooking of ingredients. It is reported to have been the favourite meal of Jonathan Swift, author of Gulliver's Travels. It came about as an excuse for the Irish to make meals out of other older meals. So the ingredients for this recipe will be whatever in the back of the fridge i guess. But if you need a bit of a guide...

1. Preheat the oven to 350°F (180°C).
2. In a large pot, cook the sausages over medium heat until browned on all sides. Remove from the pot and set aside.
3. Add the diced bacon to the pot and cook until crispy. Remove from the pot and set aside.
4. Layer the sliced potatoes and onions in the bottom of a large ovenproof casserole dish.
5. Place the sausages and bacon on top of the potato and onion layer.
6. Pour the chicken stock over the sausage and bacon mixture.
7. Season with salt and black pepper to taste.
8. Cover the casserole dish with a lid and place it in the preheated oven. Bake for 1 1/2 to 2 hours, or until the potatoes are tender.
9. Remove the casserole from the oven and sprinkle fresh parsley over the top before serving.

FARMHOUSE APPLE CAKE

SERVES
8

METHOD
OVEN

TIME
1hour 40mins

DIFFICULTY
4/10

Imagine a crisp autumn evening, the wind howling outside, and a cozy fire crackling in the hearth. What better way to warm your soul than with a slice of Irish Apple Cake? This isn't just a generations-old family recipe, it's a hug in a dessert form. Picture a golden cake cradling plump, tender apples that mingle their sweetness with a rich, buttery batter. The secret weapon? A delightful streusel topping. A generous sprinkle of brown sugar and cinnamon creates a perfectly caramelized and crunchy crown, offering a delightful textural contrast to the soft cake and apples.

INGREDIENTS:

2 1/2 cups plain flour
150g butter, chilled, chopped
3/4 cup caster sugar, plus 1/4 cup extra
2 tsp baking powder
1/2 tsp ground cinnamon
4 Granny Smith apples
2 eggs
1/4 cup milk
Vanilla custard or double cream, to serve

1. Preheat oven to 180C/160C fan forced. Invert base of a 22cm (base size) round springform pan. Grease the base with melted butter then line with baking paper. Secure the base back in pan, allowing paper to overhang the edge. Grease side of pan.
2. Place the flour and butter in a large bowl. Use your fingertips to rub the butter into the flour until the mixture resembles fine crumbs. Add the sugar, baking powder and cinnamon. Stir until well combined. Add the apple and stir until well combined. Whisk together the eggs and milk in a jug. Pour the egg mixture into the flour mixture and stir until well combined. Spoon the cake mixture into prepared pan. Use the back of a spoon to firmly press and spread mixture over base. Sprinkle the top with the extra sugar.
3. Bake for 1 hour 10 minutes or until a skewer inserted into centre comes out clean. Set aside in the pan for 10 minutes to cool slightly. Transfer to serving plate and serve with custard or cream.

ANCIENT
RAPA NUI

Welcome to the fascinating world of ancient Easter Island cuisine! The indigenous people of Rapa Nui, or Easter Island, developed a unique culinary tradition that was influenced by the island's isolated location and the limited resources available to them.

One of the most important ingredients in Easter Island cuisine was seafood, particularly fish, which was abundant in the waters surrounding the island. The Rapa Nui people used a variety of fishing techniques, such as nets and harpoons, to catch fish, which they cooked over open fires or wrapped in leaves and roasted in earth ovens.

Another staple in Easter Island cuisine was taro, a starchy root vegetable that was brought to the island by Polynesian settlers. The Rapa Nui people also cultivated sweet potatoes and yams, which were often roasted or boiled and served with fish or other seafood.

One of the most distinctive features of Easter Island cuisine was its use of wild birds, such as terns and petrels, which were caught using nets and slingshots. The birds were then cooked over open fires or roasted in earth ovens and served with vegetables and seafood.

If you want to explore the unique flavours of ancient Easter Island cuisine, there are plenty of delicious dishes to try. One popular dish is poisson cru, a raw fish salad that is marinated in lime juice and coconut milk. Another popular dish is umu, a feast that is cooked in an underground oven and features a variety of meats, vegetables, and seafood.

So come and discover the rich and flavourful world of ancient Easter Island cuisine. Whether you're looking for fresh seafood, starchy vegetables, or unique bird dishes, Easter Island cuisine is sure to delight your taste buds and transport you to a land of history and culture.

Did you know...
Birdman Cult: A Soaring Competition: While the giant Moai statues are the most iconic image of Easter Island, another fascinating aspect of their culture was the Birdman Cult. Competing chiefs or clans would send representatives to capture the first sooty tern egg of the season. This dangerous competition involved swimming to a small, rocky islet and retrieving the egg without harming the bird. The winner's chief gained prestige and religious authority for their clan.

SERVES

2

METHOD

PAN

TIME

20 mins

DIFFICULTY

2/10

INGREDIENTS:

2 cups of cooked taro root or sweet potato, mashed
1/2 cup of coconut milk
1 tbsp of honey
1/4 tsp of ground cinnamon
1/4 tsp of ground ginger
1/4 tsp of salt
1/2 cup of diced pineapple
1/2 cup of diced mango
1/4 cup of toasted coconut flakes
Optional:
sliced bananas or other tropical fruits for garnish

Escape to the tropics with this vibrant breakfast bowl! Creamy mashed taro root or sweet potato forms the base, infused with warming spices like cinnamon and ginger. A touch of coconut milk adds richness, while a vibrant medley of diced pineapple and mango bursts with juicy sweetness. Toasted coconut flakes provide a delightful textural contrast, and the entire dish is a celebration of Polynesian flavors. Enjoy this island-inspired creation on its own or with a side of fresh berries for a complete and satisfying breakfast.

1. Start by mashing the cooked taro root or sweet potato in a bowl until it's smooth and creamy.
2. Add the coconut milk, honey, cinnamon, ginger, and salt to the mashed taro or sweet potato, and stir well to combine.
3. Heat the mixture in a saucepan over medium heat, stirring constantly, until it's warmed through and well combined.
4. Divide the taro or sweet potato mixture between two bowls.
5. Top each bowl with diced pineapple and mango, and sprinkle with toasted coconut flakes.
6. Optional: Garnish the breakfast with sliced bananas or other tropical fruits if desired.
7. Serve the breakfast hot, with a side of fresh fruit or berries if desired.

Quote...
"Easter Island is a metaphor for our own planet. We are all on an island, with finite resources, and we need to learn from the mistakes of the past."
- Jared Diamond

SERVES	METHOD	TIME	DIFFICULTY
LOADS	PIT	4 hours	8/10

The Umu Pae, an underground earth oven. Imagine parcels of the freshest tuna, carefully wrapped in banana leaves and nestled amongst hot stones. These volcanic stones, heated by fire, gently cook the fish, imbuing it with a smoky essence and an incredibly moist, flaky texture. Unlike modern grilling or pan-searing, this ancient technique preserves the tuna's natural sweetness and delicate flavour.

INGREDIENTS:

1 large fresh tuna, cleaned and gutted
2-3 banana leaves
2-3 large taro leaves
2-3 sweet potatoes, peeled and sliced
1 onion, sliced
1 red bell pepper, sliced
1 green bell pepper, sliced
2 garlic cloves, minced
2 limes, juiced
2 tablespoons olive oil
Salt and pepper to taste

1. Dig a hole in the ground and start a fire using wood or charcoal, letting it burn for at least 1 hour until the rocks around the fire are hot.
2. Meanwhile, season the tuna with salt, pepper, minced garlic, lime juice, and olive oil. Allow it to marinate for at least 30 minutes.
3. Wrap the tuna in banana leaves, and then wrap it again with the taro leaves.
4. Place the wrapped tuna on the hot rocks and cover it with sweet potato slices, onion, and bell peppers.
5. Cover the entire oven with more banana and taro leaves and then cover it with dirt, making sure no steam can escape.
6. Let it cook for about 2-3 hours, depending on the size of the tuna.
7. After the cooking time has elapsed, remove the dirt and the leaves, and carefully unwrap the tuna.
8. Serve with additional lime wedges and a side of cooked vegetables or potatoes.

This unique dish has been a part of Easter Island's cuisine for centuries and is still enjoyed by locals and tourists alike.

Would you rather
Cross the Pacific in a canoe or cross the desert on a camel?

SERVES

LOADS

METHOD

PIT

TIME

4 hours

DIFFICULTY

6/10

INGREDIENTS:

Whole pig or lamb

Root vegetables such as taro, sweet potato, and cassava

Banana leaves

Coconut milk

Salt

Umu was traditionally cooked for special occasions, such as weddings or important ceremonies. It was considered a communal feast, and everyone in the village would gather around the umu to share the food and celebrate together. Today, umu is still a popular dish in Polynesian cultures, and it is often served at luaus and other festive events.

The Umu, is a traditional Polynesian feast cooked in a pit dug in the ground. The meats become incredibly tender, practically falling off the bone. The smoky kiss infuses everything with a unique depth of flavour, while the natural wrapping keeps the moisture locked in, creating a symphony of textures unlike any other.

1. Dig a large hole in the ground and line it with rocks.
2. Build a fire in the hole and let it burn until the rocks are hot.
3. Place the whole pig or lamb on top of the hot rocks and cover it with banana leaves.
4. Layer the root vegetables on top of the meat and cover them with more banana leaves.
5. Pour coconut milk over the top of the banana leaves and sprinkle with salt.
6. Cover the entire oven with more banana leaves and then with a layer of dirt.
7. Let the umu cook for several hours, until the meat is tender and the vegetables are cooked through.
8. Uncover the oven and remove the food.
9. Serve the meat and vegetables hot, garnished with fresh herbs and more coconut milk.

SERVES

4

METHOD

POT

TIME

30 mins

DIFFICULTY

2/10

Imagine a steaming bowl cradling a thick, earthy-colored mash (get purple Taro if you can). Don't let appearances deceive you! Popoi is a revelation – surprisingly light and fluffy, with a subtle sweetness and a hint of delightful tang. This Polynesian gem is crafted from taro, a starchy root vegetable that has sustained islanders for centuries and this sweetened dessert is merely one way it can be prepared. Taro boasts a unique flavour profile – almost nutty, unlike anything you've likely encountered before.

Popoi's simplicity belies its significance. It's a window into the rich history and unwavering spirit of Easter Island. Popoi is a must-try for the adventurous eater, a gateway to the extraordinary flavours of Easter Island. Who knows, it might just become your new favourite comfort food!

INGREDIENTS:

1kg (2lb) taro root

2 cups coconut milk

1 cup water

1 cup sugar

Banana leaves for serving

1. Peel the taro root and cut it into small pieces.
2. In a large pot, boil the taro root with enough water to cover it until it is tender.
3. Drain the taro root and mash it with a potato masher or fork.
4. In a separate pot, heat the coconut milk, water, and sugar until the sugar has dissolved.
5. Add the mashed taro root to the coconut milk mixture and stir until well combined.
6. Serve the popoi in small bowls or wrapped in banana leaves. Enjoy this traditional Easter Island dessert!

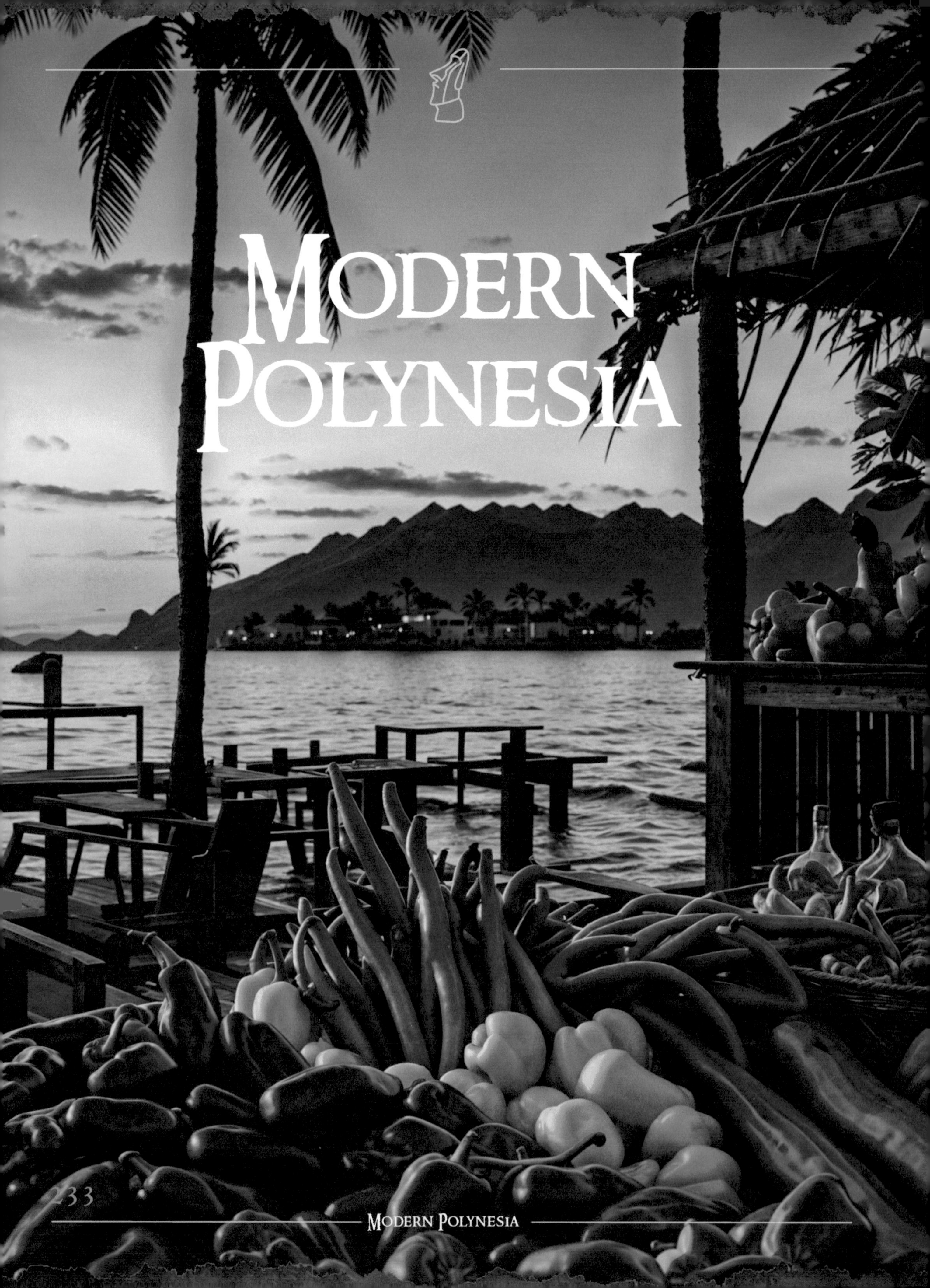

Modern Polynesia

Today, Polynesian cuisine has been influenced by a variety of factors, including colonialism, immigration, and globalisation. While traditional dishes still hold an important place in Polynesian culture, you can also find modern twists and international flavours.

One of the most popular Polynesian dishes is poke, a Hawaiian dish made with raw fish, usually tuna, marinated in soy sauce and sesame oil. Other popular dishes include kalua pig, a Hawaiian dish made by roasting a whole pig in an underground oven, and kokoda, a Fijian dish made with raw fish marinated in coconut milk and lime juice.

Polynesian cuisine is unique in its use of fresh, local ingredients. Each island has its own specialties, such as taro in Samoa, breadfruit in Tonga, and yams in Fiji. Coconut is a staple ingredient in many Polynesian dishes, used in everything from curries to desserts.

Another unique aspect of Polynesian cuisine is its connection to the land and sea. Many Polynesians still practice traditional fishing and farming methods, and the use of sustainable, locally sourced ingredients is emphasised. Despite modern influences, Polynesian cuisine still holds onto its traditional roots. Many families continue to use recipes that have been passed down for generations and traditional dishes are often served at special occasions such as weddings and festivals.

Overall, Polynesian cuisine is a delicious fusion of ancient and modern flavours, with an emphasis on fresh, locally sourced ingredients and a deep connection to the land and sea. Whether you're a seasoned cook or a beginner, there's no shortage of delicious flavours to explore in Polynesian cooking. So grab some fresh fish, coconut, and taro, and get ready to experience the unique and delicious world of Polynesian cuisine!

Did you know...
Va'a: More Than Just Canoes, They're Racing Royalty: Traditional Polynesian voyaging canoes, known as va'a, haven't been relegated to museums. Va'a racing is a hugely popular sport across Polynesia, with competitions drawing teams from various islands. These races test the paddlers' strength, teamwork, and connection to their seafaring heritage. The atmosphere is electric, with vibrant team colours and enthusiastic drumming adding to the excitement.

LOCO MOCO

SERVES
4

METHOD
PAN

TIME
25mins

DIFFICULTY
2/10

INGREDIENTS:

450g (1lb) ground beef
2 cloves garlic, minced
Salt and black pepper to taste
4 cups cooked white rice
4 large eggs
1/4 cup flour
1/4 cup butter
2 cups beef broth
2 tbsp soy sauce
2 tbsp Worcestershire sauce
2 tbsp cornstarch
2 tbsp water
Sliced green onions, for garnish

You've just kicked back after a day surfing the perfect Hawaiian waves. Your stomach's rumbling for something satisfying, but the thought of a heavy meal feels overwhelming. Enter Loco Moco, my island go-to for comfort food with a kick.

1. In a large bowl, mix together the ground beef, minced garlic, salt, and black pepper. Shape the mixture into four hamburger patties.
2. Heat a large skillet over medium-high heat. Cook the hamburger patties for about 5-6 minutes on each side, or until browned and cooked through.
3. While the hamburger patties are cooking, prepare the gravy. In a small saucepan, melt the butter over medium heat. Add the flour and whisk to combine.
4. Slowly pour in the beef broth, whisking constantly until the mixture is smooth. Add the soy sauce and Worcestershire sauce, and continue whisking until the gravy thickens.
5. In a separate small bowl, mix the cornstarch and water together until smooth. Add the mixture to the gravy and continue whisking until the gravy thickens even more.
6. In another skillet, fry the eggs until the whites are set but the yolks are still runny.
7. To assemble the loco moco, place a scoop of cooked white rice onto a plate. Place a hamburger patty on top of the rice, and then place a fried egg on top of the hamburger patty.
8. Pour the gravy over the top of the loco moco and garnish with sliced green onions.
9. Repeat the process for the remaining servings.

Quote...
"The oral traditions of the Pacific Islands are rich with stories of bravery, resourcefulness, and overcoming challenges. These stories inspire future generations and keep their history alive."
- Édouard Glissant

HAWAIIAN CHICKEN

SERVES
4

METHOD
OVEN

TIME
45mins

DIFFICULTY
2/10

These sticky Hawaiian Chicken drumsticks are marinated with a pineapple-based glaze that is sweet, spicy and slightly tangy. Accompanied by a coconut rice that is so delicious I could eat a giant bowl of it for lunch on its own. It puts me in a good mood just making them! I mean, how much more tropical can you get than chicken with a pineapple marinade and coconut rice on the side?

1. Preheat oven to 375°F.
2. Season the chicken breasts with salt and pepper, and place them in a 9x13 inch baking dish.
3. In a bowl, whisk together the coconut milk, soy sauce, brown sugar, apple cider vinegar, garlic, and ginger.
4. Pour the coconut milk mixture over the chicken, making sure to coat each piece.
5. Scatter the pineapple chunks around the chicken.
6. Bake the chicken for 25-30 minutes, or until it is cooked through and the sauce is bubbly.
7. In a small bowl, whisk together the cornstarch and cold water.
8. Remove the chicken from the oven, and pour the sauce into a small saucepan.
9. Whisk the cornstarch slurry into the saucepan, and bring the sauce to a simmer.
10. Cook the sauce, whisking constantly, until it has thickened.
11. Pour the thickened sauce back over the chicken.
12. Serve the Hawaiian chicken over cooked rice, and garnish with sliced green onions and sesame seeds.

INGREDIENTS:

4 boneless, skinless chicken breasts
1 can coconut milk
1 cup canned pineapple chunks, drained
1/4 cup low-sodium soy sauce
1/4 cup brown sugar
2 tbsp apple cider vinegar
2 garlic cloves, minced
1 tsp grated ginger
Salt and pepper
2 tbsp cornstarch
1/4 cup cold water
Cooked rice, for serving
Sliced green onions, for garnish
Sesame seeds, for garnish

Would you rather...
Stay in the best 5-star hotel in Hawaii or stay in an authentic untouched village on an isolated island?

POLYNESIAN MEATBALLS

SERVES
4

METHOD
OVEN

TIME
45mins

DIFFICULTY
2/10

INGREDIENTS:

For the meatballs:
450g (1lb) ground beef
1/2 cup breadcrumbs
1/4 cup milk
1 egg
1/4 cup finely chopped onion
1 tsp salt
1/4 tsp black pepper
1/4 tsp garlic powder
1/4 tsp ground ginger
1 tbsp soy sauce

For the sauce:
1 cup pineapple juice
1/4 cup brown sugar
1/4 cup rice vinegar
1/4 cup ketchup
1 tbsp soy sauce
1/2 tsp ground ginger
1/4 tsp garlic powder

For serving:
Cooked white rice
Sliced green onions

The sweetness of pineapple, the savoury richness of soy sauce, and a touch of playful spice. It's a Hawaiian twist on a classic comfort food, with an extra layer of tropical sunshine.These beauties aren't just delicious, for those who grew up with them, they evoke childhood memories of family gatherings and island vacations.

1. Preheat the oven to 400°F (200°C) and line a baking sheet with parchment paper.
2. In a large bowl, combine the ground beef, breadcrumbs, milk, egg, onion, salt, black pepper, garlic powder, ginger, and soy sauce. Mix until well combined.
3. Shape the mixture into small meatballs, about 1 inch in diameter, and place them on the prepared baking sheet.
4. Bake the meatballs for 20-25 minutes, until cooked through and lightly browned.
5. While the meatballs are baking, prepare the sauce. In a medium saucepan, combine the pineapple juice, brown sugar, rice vinegar, ketchup, soy sauce, ginger, and garlic powder. Bring to a simmer over medium heat and cook for 10-12 minutes, until slightly thickened.
6. When the meatballs are cooked, transfer them to the saucepan with the sauce and stir gently to coat.
7. Serve the meatballs and sauce over cooked white rice, and sprinkle with sliced green onions.

HAUPIA

SERVES	METHOD	TIME	DIFFICULTY
4	POT	2hours	2/10

Imagine this: you've just conquered the lush rainforests of Kauai. The sun-kissed skin and salty breeze leave you craving something cool, refreshing, and bursting with islandy goodness. Look no further than Haupia, a vibrant coconut dessert that captures the essence of paradise in every bite. Silky smooth coconut milk pudding, infused with the comforting warmth of vanilla and flecked with toasted coconut flakes for a delightful textural contrast. Lighter than cheesecake but just as satisfying.

1. In a medium saucepan, whisk together the coconut milk, sugar, and cornstarch until smooth.
2. Heat the mixture over medium heat, whisking constantly, until it simmers and thickens. This will take about 5-7 minutes.
3. The mixture should coat the back of a spoon.
4. If using, stir in the vanilla extract.
5. Pour the haupia mixture into a 20 x 20 cm baking dish or loaf pan.
6. Cover the surface of the haupia directly with plastic wrap to prevent a skin from forming. Let it cool completely at room temperature for at least 2 hours, or refrigerate for at least 4 hours until set.
7. To serve, cut the haupia into squares and garnish with toasted coconut flakes if desired.

INGREDIENTS:

1 can full-fat coconut milk (not coconut cream)

1/2 cup granulated sugar

2 tbsp cornstarch

1/2 cup water

1 tsp vanilla extract (optional)

1/4 cup toasted coconut flakes, for garnish (optional)

Made in the USA
Columbia, SC
11 November 2024

c9bd8b66-9d9a-4649-9ae9-dedd0a4e94a6R01